BLACK SCIENTISTS

A M E R I C A N

P R O F I L E S

BLACK SCIENTISTS

■

Lisa Yount

Facts On File
New York • Oxford

Black Scientists

Copyright © 1991 by Lisa Yount

For information contact:

Facts On File, Inc.
460 Park Avenue South
New York NY 10016
USA

Facts On File Limited
Collins Street
Oxford OX4 1XJ
United Kingdom

61 499

Library of Congress Cataloging-in-Publication Data

Yount, Lisa
    Black Scientists
      p. cm. — (American profiles series)
    Includes bibliographical references and index.
    Summary: Profiles Afro-Americans who made important contributions
    to science despite racial prejudice and institutional barriers to
    black education and achievement.
    ISBN 0-8160-2549-5
    1. Afro-American scientists—United States—Biography—Juvenile
literature. 2. Science—United States—History—20th century—
Juvenile literature. [1. Scientists. 2. Afro-Americans—
Biography.] I. Title. II. Series.
Q141. Y68 1991
500 '.89'96073—dc20
[920]
[B]   90-19159

A British CIP catalogue record for this book is available from the British Library.

Facts On File books are available at special discounts when purchased in bulk quantities for businesses, associations, institutions or sales promotions. Please contact our Special Sales Department in New York at 212/683-2244 (dial 800/322-8755 except in NY, AK, or HI) or in Oxford at 865/728399.

Text design by Ron Monteleone
Jacket design by Ron Monteleone
Composition by Facts On File, Inc.
Manufactured by the Maple-Vail Book Manufacturing Group
Printed in the United States of America

10 9 8 7 6 5 4 3 2 1

This book is printed on acid-free paper.

Contents

Introduction vii

Daniel Hale Williams 1

George Washington Carver 14

Ernest Everett Just 28

Percy Lavon Julian 41

Charles Richard Drew 54

Jane Cooke Wright 67

Bertram O. Fraser-Reid 80

John P. Moon 94

Index 107

For Trisha and Chris
with love from Aunt Lisa

Introduction

Mastering a field of science is a task difficult enough to challenge anyone. All the people profiled in this book, however, faced another challenge as well: they were black. Until the last few decades, having dark skin made a scientific career in the United States almost impossible. Only a handful of extremely talented and determined people managed to overcome this double challenge and make important advances in pure or applied science. This book is more about what these people succeeded in doing than about the difficulties they faced, but being black unavoidably shaped all their lives to some extent.

It should be no surprise that all the scientists described in this book did their important work in the 20th (or very late 19th) century. Until the beginning of this century—and, sadly, well beyond that time in many places—most white Americans doubted that blacks possessed even ordinary intelligence, let alone the special brilliance of a top-notch scientist. Many believed blacks to be a separate, more or less subhuman species. Doubt of black intelligence was shared even by such enlightened men as Thomas Jefferson.

Before the Thirteenth Amendment ended slavery in the United States in 1865, many American blacks were slaves. They generally were denied even the most basic education. Some slaves' hands were cut off when their masters learned that they could write.

Freedom did not improve the situation much. Blacks usually could go to school only with other blacks, and black schools were almost always inferior. Even if a talented black person somehow gained a first-class education, there was almost nothing that he ("she" was almost unheard of) could do with it. Edward Bouchet (1852–1918), the first American black to obtain a Ph.D. degree, won that degree (in physics, in 1876) from no less an institution than Yale University—yet the only career open to him was teaching in black high schools.

Black leaders in the early years of the 20th century were divided about the best approach to take toward educating blacks and improving their position in society. Booker T. Washington, head of Tuskegee Institute in Alabama, was the leading spokesperson for one of these views. He believed that black educators, even at the college level, should concentrate on teaching vocational rather than academic subjects. Providing blacks with advanced scientific training was a waste of time, he felt, since this training could not be used. Washington's views on education were part of a larger belief that black people could improve their lives only by accepting and working within the discriminatory social system that surrounded them. "Cast down your bucket where you are"—that is, make the best of one's existing circumstances—was one of Washington's favorite phrases. He believed that if blacks worked hard, demonstrated their ability, and were patient, the social system would slowly change.

Another black leader, W.E.B. DuBois, held exactly the opposite view. He believed that blacks' lives would be improved only by challenging the unjust social system at every turn. He urged that the "talented tenth"—those young blacks who showed the highest abilities—be given the best education possible. He expected that these young people would then become leaders who would bring blacks as a whole to a better life.

These opposing views had powerful effects on the lives of the black scientists who worked in the early 20th century. George Washington Carver taught at Tuskegee Institute and shared Booker Washington's views about the education of blacks. Carver concentrated on helping and educating "the man farthest down," the poor black southern farmer. Most of his many speeches and writings presented simple ideas that promised to be of immediate practical use.

Ernest Everett Just, by contrast, was in some ways a perfect representative of DuBois's "talented tenth." A man as proud as he was brilliant, Just pursued a career in pure science against all odds and demanded completely equal and unprejudiced treatment from everyone he met. Yet in other ways, Just was as far from DuBois's ideal as Carver was. Just resented having to teach in a black university that could offer him no money for laboratory equipment or time for the research he loved. (By contrast, some other black scientists, such as Daniel Williams and Charles Drew, were devoted teachers who were happy to concentrate their energies on making the graduates of black universities and medical schools the equal of, as Drew said, "anyone, anywhere.")

As Percy Julian, whose career overlapped Just's in time and who encountered many of the same problems, pointed out, Just's seemingly selfish attitude showed a flaw not in Just but in what was expected of black scientists. "Historically the Negro student of science has not been able to enjoy the luxury of exclusive devotion to his discipline," Julian wrote in a 1969 essay. "He was expected, strangely enough by his colleagues of both races, to . . . becom[e] involved in social problems, which no one expected of his white fellow scientists."

Like the careers of Charles Drew and other black scientists who worked around the middle of the 20th century, Julian's career reflected a mixture of disappointment and hope. In his early years as a scientist, Julian, like Just, bitterly resented being confined to black colleges in the United States and sought better training and treatment in Europe. Unlike Just, however, Julian returned to the United States and went on to achieve both a faculty post (though one with no possibility of advancement) in a white college and success in industry.

Julian's own success and that of others—as well as, no doubt, the successes of the civil rights movement in the 1960s—led Julian to see hope for future black American scientists. "The ghetto gloom of apartheid [legal segregation] is slowly but surely fading on the horizon," he wrote in 1969. "The Negro scientist now need neither starve nor be condemned to a frustrating intellectual ghetto if he chooses pure science as a career."

Obviously it would be foolish to claim that race prejudice has vanished from American society, or even from American academic and business life. Nonetheless, the careers of the three most recent scientists in this book seem to bear out Julian's optimistic words. Jane Wright, Bertram Fraser-Reid, and John Moon all deny that being black held back their work in any significant way. Fraser-Reid and Moon both say that talent is likely to be far more important than race in determining a young scientist's success today, whether that person enters the academic or the business world. "If you contribute," Moon says, "you play."

American society's reaction to the achievements of black scientists has differed as much as the reactions of the scientists themselves to being black. On the one hand, until recently society withheld official recognition and positions of power from black scientists because of their race. On the other hand, at times it has glorified the names of certain scientists seemingly far out of proportion to their achievements precisely because they are black.

Benjamin Banneker, an 18th-century scientist known for his knowledge of astronomy and his almanacs, is one example. There can be no doubt of Banneker's abilities. Had he lived in a later time, he might well have made important discoveries in mathematics or astronomy. Nonetheless, there also can be no question that his work did not advance science in any way that should have brought lasting fame. Other people were excellent surveyors or calculated astronomical tables for almanacs as accurately as Banneker did, and today most of their names are, at best, footnotes in specialized history books. Yet Banneker became, and to some extent has remained, famous.

George Washington Carver is perhaps the most striking example of such treatment. Carver biographer Linda McMurry has written, "Perhaps the greatest paradox [of Carver's career] was that Carver became famous as a scientist because he was black, even though his blackness diverted him from becoming a real scientist. If he had been white, he probably would have made significant contributions in mycology [the study of the plantlike living things called fungi] or hybridization [the crossbreeding of plants] and died in obscurity [unknown]. Because he was black, he died famous, without making any significant scientific advances." McMurry goes on to point out, however, that Carver did have ideas about nature that are widely shared among scientists today, though they were not appreciated in his time.

Motives for giving some black scientists more credit than their due have varied. Many people who did this had good intentions. Black groups wanted to show shining examples of black achievement. Liberal whites, similarly, wished to praise the accomplishments of a group who unquestionably had had to work under difficult circumstances. Some other groups had less noble motives, however. George Washington Carver may have won such high praise at least partly because his humble behavior, focus on helping the poor, and unwillingness to challenge southern society presented the sort of image that some whites hoped other blacks would imitate. Other whites may have praised black scientists either to suggest that society really did not prevent black advancement or to ease feelings of guilt about the way blacks had been treated. When accepting an award as "Chicagoan of the Year" in 1950, Percy Julian stated bluntly, "Friends, I appreciate deeply all this outpouring of good will, but I don't know why you should so honor me, except that I belong to a race which hangs heavily on your consciences."

Whatever the motives for this kind of exaggeration, it has led to the development and wide acceptance of certain "myths" about the most famous black scientists. Some writers, especially writers for children and young people, could not resist making a good story better and included completely fictional incidents in their biographies of these scientists. Later writers unknowingly passed on these stories as fact.

Other "myths" probably have arisen at least as much from misunderstandings about science as from misunderstandings about blacks. It is both easier and more impressive to say that someone is "the one" or "the first" to make a discovery than to attempt to explain that someone added—even though significantly—to a store of knowledge that was begun before that person worked, added to by others at the same time as his or her achievements, and continued by still others after the person's work was completed. Thus it has been widely reported that George Washington Carver almost singlehandedly "saved" southern agriculture and that Charles Drew "invented" blood banks or the use of blood plasma in transfusions. Percy Julian said that he grew very tired of having to deny that he was "the discoverer of cortisone." A book about individuals, like this one, unavoidably emphasizes individual achievements, but I have tried to define those achievements as accurately as possible.

Because black scientists have faced special difficulties during most of the United States's history, it is still worthwhile to single them out. Those difficulties have united them to some extent. Nonetheless, as Bertram Fraser-Reid points out, the scientific world of today is interracial and international. When future books about scientists and the history of science are written, they probably will pay little attention to factors such as race and sex. I believe, however, that such books will include the names of at least some of the scientists described here. Their achievements are indeed the equal of those of "anyone, anywhere."

Daniel Hale Williams
(1856–1931)

*Daniel Hale Williams. Williams performed
the first successful surgery on the heart
and founded the country's first
interracial hospital.*
(Courtesy Moorland-Spingarn Research Center,
Howard University.)

*T*he anesthetized patient lies on the operating table. As in any modern operating room, the cloths covering the patient's body, the metal instruments on a tray nearby, and the clothing and masks worn by the surgeons and nurses have all been sterilized, or made completely free of microorganisms that might cause infection.

With a swift motion the chief surgeon cuts open the patient's chest. The surgeon connects a major vein and a major artery to a heart-lung machine. Blood from the vein will be pumped through the machine repeatedly and resupplied each time with oxygen before being returned to the patient's body through the artery. Once the machine is doing the heart's work, the surgeon can stop the heart and begin to operate. Depending on the patient's need, the surgeon may replace fat-blocked arteries that have caused a heart attack, cut tiny holes in the heart with a laser to increase blood flow in the heart muscle, or even replace the heart with one provided by a donor.

Surgery was very different a little over a hundred years ago. Doctors operated in long, swallow-tailed black coats. Nurses wore street clothes. Patients were lucky if the doctors remembered to wash their hands before beginning an operation. Anesthesia was used, but it was crude, and its fumes often made the surgeons almost as sleepy as the patient. X-rays, antibiotics, and blood transfusions, let alone heart-lung machines and lasers, did not exist. Many patients died of infection after even minor surgery. Because of the risk of infection, surgeons opened a patient's abdomen only as a last resort. They almost never opened the chest.

Under conditions only a little better than this, Daniel Hale Williams, a black doctor, performed the first successful surgery on the heart. He succeeded where others had failed because he was willing to follow the newest and best ideas in surgery and was bold enough to go a little beyond what anyone else had tried. Those same characteristics brought him success when he founded the country's first interracial hospital and first training school for black nurses.

Daniel Hale Williams was born in Hollidaysburg, Pennsylvania, on January 18, 1856. His parents, Daniel Williams, Jr., and Sarah Price Williams, were free people of mixed white, black, and Indian ancestry.

Daniel Williams, Jr., a barber, died when young Dan was 11. Leaving Dan as an apprentice to a shoemaker in Baltimore, Maryland, Sarah Williams moved to Rockford, Illinois. Dan had no desire to be a shoemaker, however. After a year he left that job and began to make his own way. Sometimes he worked as a waiter on steamboats on the Great Lakes, and occasionally he earned money by singing and playing the guitar. For a while when he was 17 he had his own barbershop in Edgerton, a small Wisconsin town. Soon, however, he moved to a larger nearby town, Janesville, and went to work for a black barber named Charles Henry (Harry) Anderson. Dan lived with Mr. and Mrs. Anderson and was treated like a member of the family.

Dan remembered his father insisting, "We colored people must cultivate the mind." Following this advice, Dan enrolled in Janesville's Classical Academy. After graduating in 1877, he studied law for a year but then stopped because, he said, he didn't like making money from other people's quarrels. He became interested in medicine after meeting a well-known local doctor named Henry Palmer. He became Palmer's apprentice, helping the doctor do his work in exchange for being taught the skills of medicine. Being an apprentice to an established doctor was the normal first step in medical training in those days.

In 1880 Dan and two other apprentices of Palmer's went to Chicago Medical College, one of the best medical schools in the country at the time, to continue their training. Dan had saved a little money and worked part time, but he had to borrow most of the money for his medical education from Harry Anderson.

Surgery was the part of medicine that interested Dan most, and the early 1880s were an exciting time to become a surgeon. The ideas of the British surgeon Joseph Lister were beginning to change completely the way operations were done. Starting in the late 1850s, Louis Pasteur, a Frenchman, had shown that many forms of disease were caused by minute living germs (bacteria or other microorganisms). Lister concluded that the often-fatal sepsis, or infection, that usually followed injuries or surgical operations also was caused by germs. If germs could be kept away from surgical wounds, he thought, infection might be prevented.

Lister found that carbolic acid, a powerful and strong-smelling chemical, killed germs. If he treated wounds with carbolic acid, infection did not develop. In the 1860s he began to use carbolic acid in surgery as well. Before operating he washed his hands and soaked his surgical instruments in the irritating liquid. During an operation an assistant sprayed the patient, the surgeon, the dressings, and everything else in the room with suffocating carbolic acid mist. At first other surgeons, many of whom either had not heard of Pasteur's ideas or did not believe them, thought that Lister's actions were almost insane. Slowly, however, they realized that their patients were still dying of infection but Lister's were not. Lister's ideas about antiseptic surgery—surgery done in a way that reduced or prevented infection—began to be accepted.

When Dan Williams watched his first surgical operations in medical school, Lister's ideas were still considered controversial and experimental. Williams's surgery professor, Edmund Andrews, believed in them, however. Williams soon did, too.

Daniel Hale Williams received his medical degree in March of 1883. "Dr. Dan," as his many patients called him, became a popular and prosperous doctor. In addition to his private practice, he served as the doctor for the Protestant Orphan Asylum and worked on the surgical staff of the South Side Dispensary. He also taught at Chicago Medical College. In 1889 the governor of Illinois appointed him to the state's Board of Health.

Williams sometimes operated on his patients in their homes. This happened partly because many hospitals either refused to treat black people or accepted them only in filthy charity wards. It also happened because many sick people, both black and white, were afraid of hospitals and refused to enter them for treatment.

When Williams operated in a home, he insisted on having everything as clean as possible. Walls and floors had to be scrubbed. He draped the "operating room"—often the dining room, with the patient lying on the dinner table—with freshly laundered white sheets. He kept a kettle of water boiling on the kitchen stove to sterilize his instruments.

One chilly evening in December 1890, Williams was introduced to Emma Reynolds, the sister of a Chicago minister. Reynolds, an intelligent and ambitious young woman, wanted to become a nurse. None of the few American nursing schools then in existence, however, would accept a black woman. The minister, Reverend Louis Reynolds, asked Williams to help his sister find a place to train.

Emma Reynolds's problem was related to others that Williams already had been thinking about. The idea of trained nurses was just as new and controversial as the idea of antiseptic surgery. Williams wanted to see nurses, both white and black, trained to high standards and taught the newest ideas about cleanliness. He also wanted to see training for doctors, especially black surgeons, improved. At that time, even if a black surgeon went to a good medical school, he was not allowed to operate in most hospitals. He thus could not get practical experience or find steady work on a hospital staff. Finally, Williams wanted to see hospitals that treated black patients with the dignity they deserved.

All these needs could be met by starting a new hospital, Williams told the startled minister and his sister on that December night.

The hospital would be run mostly by and for black people, but it would be open to doctors and patients of all races. It would include a school that would provide black nurses with the best in modern training. Young black doctors, too, could gain practical experience there.

Williams began to spread his idea among his many friends. Some Chicago blacks opposed him because they feared that his hospital would be an inferior "separate" facility, but Williams reminded them that patients and doctors would be both black and white. More and more people of both races, rich and poor, came to support Williams's plan. The rich donated money, and the others sent what they could: beds, sheets, soap, even homemade jelly and loaves of bread.

The Provident Hospital and Training School opened its doors on May 4, 1891. It was the country's first interracial hospital and first training school for black nurses. At first it had only 12 beds. Small as Provident was, however, Williams insisted on high standards for it from the beginning. Only doctors from accredited medical schools were allowed to practice there. Only the most intelligent and well-educated young women were accepted by the nurses' school. They trained for 18 months, following a rigorous course. Williams's care paid off. Of the 189 people treated at Provident during its first year, only 22 died. This was a very good record for any hospital of the time, since only the sickest or most severely injured people went to a hospital.

Many of Provident's patients were injury victims, and it was one of these that allowed "Dr. Dan" to make history. On July 9, 1893, a sweltering hot day, a young black man named James Cornish got into a fight in a bar and was stabbed in the chest. Williams, then Provident's chief surgeon, examined the stab wound when Cornish was brought to the hospital. The wound was about an inch long and not bleeding much. At first it did not seem too serious. But then Cornish became pale and developed a sharp, barking cough. X-rays had not been invented yet, so Williams had no way to see what was happening in Cornish's chest. He suspected, however, that the man was bleeding inside. A major blood vessel, perhaps even the heart itself, must have been cut by the knife.

Even though antiseptic surgery had become more popular and operations on the abdomen by then were fairly common, most surgeons still refused to open the chest. In addition to the danger of infection there was the risk that the lungs might collapse as air

5

rushed into the chest cavity. Even the best-known surgeons generally held that "surgical interference with the heart is impracticable." The usual treatment for suspected heart wounds, therefore, was cold packs, rest, painkillers, and perhaps prayer. If the heart really had been injured, the patient almost always died from internal bleeding.

Williams decided to operate on Cornish in the hope of saving his life. The black surgeon made an incision and then cut a sort of trap door, about two inches long and an inch and a half wide, in one rib. Through this tiny opening he peered into the chest cavity. Sure enough, he saw that one major blood vessel had been nicked by the knife. Cornish had lost enough blood to go into shock (collapse of the circulatory system, caused by loss of blood). Williams tied off this vessel so it would not bleed anymore.

Worse still, the knife had indeed touched Cornish's heart. The pericardium, or sac surrounding the heart, showed a tear an inch and a quarter long. Williams spread the edges of the tear apart and looked inside. Luckily, the heart muscle itself had barely been scratched. Its wound would need no stitches. The wound in the pericardium, however, would need to be sutured, or sewn up. This was not going to be easy because the pericardium was fluttering like a wounded bird, moving up and down with every heartbeat—130 times a minute.

Williams cleaned the wound with salt solution. Then he held the quivering edges of the pericardium together and sewed them shut with a threadlike catgut suture. The suture would be absorbed by the body as the wound healed—if infection did not set in. Finally, dripping by then with sweat, Williams closed the outer incisions.

Williams hardly left Cornish's side for the next several days. At first Cornish contracted fever, a sign of infection, but the fever fell. Three weeks later Williams had to operate again to drain bloody fluid from Cornish's chest cavity, but this was an expected complication. There was no pus in the fluid; infection in the chest had not occurred. Cornish was sent home, completely well, 51 days after he had come to the hospital. He was still alive 20 years later.

Williams did not have time to write an account of his historic operation for a medical journal until three and a half years afterward. But a Chicago newspaper, the *Inter-Ocean*, ran the story immediately. "SEWED UP HIS HEART!" the story's headline shouted. Williams found himself famous.

An opportunity for a different kind of fame came Williams's way in 1894. When President Grover Cleveland began his second term, the new administration decided to appoint a new chief surgeon for Freedmen's Hospital in Washington, D.C. Freedmen's, controlled at that time by the Department of the Interior, had been established to take care of the many poor, aged, and sick blacks who flooded into the capital city after the Civil War. The 200-bed hospital was connected with Howard University, a black college in Washington, and students at Howard's medical school took their training there. At that time Freedman's was run by a doctor, Charles B. Purvis, who knew nothing of the new surgical methods. The huge hospital had no trained nurses. Its death rate was very high.

Williams was persuaded to apply for the job of chief surgeon at Freedmen's. He won the post, but an infected leg resulting from a hunting accident kept him from going to Washington for many months. When he finally arrived in September 1894, however, he made up for lost time. He divided the disorganized hospital into seven medical departments and added two new ones, one for bacteriology and one for pathology (the study of diseased tissue).

Freedman's Hospital, Washington, D.C., around 1907. As chief surgeon of Freedmen's, Daniel Williams modernized this large government hospital for blacks and established a nurses' training school there.
(Courtesy Moorland-Spingarn Research Center, Howard University.)

He opened Freedmen's to white doctors and to black doctors not connected with Howard and set up a training program that allowed newly graduated doctors (interns) to learn from practical work in the hospital. He also set up a training program for nurses that was modeled on the one at Provident. He got an enclosed passage built between the operating room and one of the wards so that surgical patients would no longer have to be carried across an open courtyard in all kinds of weather. He set up a horse-drawn ambulance wagon with "Freedmen's Hospital" painted on the side.

By the end of Williams's first year in charge, Freedmen's was a different place. Its death rate had dropped drastically. Out of 533 surgical patients treated there during that year, only eight died.

Williams was making other changes, too. He had attended many meetings of medical societies in Chicago; that city was less strictly segregated than many, and Williams's high reputation made him welcome almost everywhere. He knew that medical societies provided an important way for doctors to exchange information about scientific advances. But black doctors were not allowed to be members of many local medical societies, and they were firmly barred from the national one, the American Medical Association. In December 1895, therefore, Williams and others established a medical society for black doctors, the National Medical Association. Williams became the association's first vice president. The group is still active today.

Williams resigned from his post at Freedmen's in February 1898. He felt he had done as much as he could for the hospital. He also was tired of the constant attacks and accusations that came from Purvis and his friends, who resented the changes that Williams had made. Williams's stay in Washington had not been entirely unpleasant, however. While there he had met an attractive schoolteacher, Alice Johnson. The 42-year-old Williams married Johnson, 39, on April 2, 1898. He then brought his new wife back to Chicago.

But Williams soon found out that he was not through with Freedmen's. In June 1898 a Board of Visitors, appointed by the Department of the Interior, made public a report that complained of bad management at the hospital. The report accused Williams of keeping poor records and even of stealing surgical instruments and other hospital supplies for his personal use.

Williams went back to Washington to answer the charges. He showed that, far from having taken instruments from the hospital, he had left some of his own behind. Most of the supposedly "missing" items had simply been used up or worn out. Williams finally was cleared of all blame, but some of his reforms were undone.

On his return to Chicago, Williams rejoined the staff of Provident Hospital. The hospital now was in a larger building, with 65 beds and a "complete and superior operating room." There Williams continued to perform groundbreaking surgery. One case in 1902, like the operation on William Cornish, resulted from a stab wound. This time the knife had damaged the spleen, an abdominal organ important to the blood system. The spleen is full of blood vessels and delicate, spongy tissue. Williams was afraid that the injured man would bleed to death if the large wound in the spleen were not sutured, but suturing a spleen was thought to be impossible. It was like trying to sew pieces of tissue paper without tearing them. Every time Williams pulled a stitch tight, it tore through the spleen tissue.

Then Williams remembered that catgut sutures swelled when they were wet. Using a curved needle, he pulled the catgut through very gently in loose stitches. Then he applied hot gauze dressings to each stitch. The catgut swelled, closing the wound. The stitches stayed put and did not tear through the tissue. The bleeding stopped, and the man's life was saved. Only one similar operation had been done successfully in the United States before.

Williams was proud of the organizational work he had done at Provident and at Freedmen's. He wanted to see high-quality medical care for black patients and training for black doctors and nurses brought to other parts of the country as well, especially to the Deep South, where they were desperately needed. One place where he was able to improve training was Meharry Medical College in Nashville. Meharry, like Howard, was one of the few schools that tried to give black doctors real medical training. Starting in 1899, Williams went to Meharry as visiting professor of clinical surgery for a week each year. His lectures and operations were always crowded with eager students.

As he had done in Chicago, Williams persuaded the black citizens of Nashville to open their own hospital. This hospital would help not only patients but the medical students of Meharry, who could get practical training there. Williams emphasized that black people should take action to solve their own problems rather than depending on white people. "Dependency on the part of the Negro has always proved a detriment [drawback]," he said. "When we have learned to do well *what we have the ability to do*, we will have accomplished much toward changing sentiments now against us."

Unfortunately, jealousy and arguments made Williams's later years at Provident as unpleasant as his years at Freedmen's had been. Most of the trouble came from a black doctor named George C. Hall. Hall had disliked Williams since Provident's first days, when Williams had refused Hall a place on the hospital's staff because he didn't think Hall's medical training was adequate. Hall later improved his training, got a minor post at Provident, and took advantage of Williams's absence at Freedmen's to work his way up in the hospital hierarchy.

When Williams was made associate attending surgeon at St. Luke's, Chicago's biggest hospital, in 1912, Hall and his friends claimed that accepting the post showed Williams's disloyalty to the black race. Hall persuaded Provident's board of directors to order Williams to send all his patients to Provident. Rather than either complying or trying to defend himself, Williams resigned from the Provident staff.

Williams continued to operate at St. Luke's and other hospitals for a number of years. He also traveled around the country as a speaker and guest surgeon. In 1913 he became the only black among the 100 charter (founding) members of the prestigious American College of Surgeons.

In 1920 Willliams and his wife retired to what had been their summer home in Idlewild, a wooded spot in northern Michigan. Alice Williams died there in 1924. Two years later Williams suffered the first of a series of strokes. He died at Idlewild on August 4, 1931.

Once when someone at Provident said something in praise of Dan Williams, George Hall was heard to shout, "Curse him! I'll punish him worse than God ever will. I'll see he's forgotten before he's dead!" For a while it seemed that Hall would succeed. In the hospital Williams had founded, his portrait was left in the basement to gather dust. One day some visitors asked what had happened to Williams and, before anyone else could reply, another visitor answered, "Oh, didn't you know? He died years ago," although in fact Williams was still alive. Both at Provident and at Freedmen's in Washington, not only Williams's fame but the strict standards of training and care he had established seemed for a while to have been forgotten.

Williams's memory was revived, however. Years after his death, the last surviving member of the group of men who had founded Provident Hospital rescued Williams's portrait and saw that it was hung in a prominent place in the hospital's new building. Most medical books also continued to list Williams as the first person to successfully sew up the heart sac. (A similar operation apparently had been performed in St. Louis in 1891, but it was not known how long the patient lived after the operation.)

Williams left other legacies as well. Provident Hospital is no longer in operation, but the model of the interracial hospital and black nursing school started by Williams led to the founding of 40 similar institutions in 20 states, many of which still survive. Howard and Meharry, the two medical schools that Williams had guided, were for many years the only two respectable medical schools for blacks. Later black surgeons such as Charles Drew, who taught at Howard and Freedmen's, were inspired to continue Williams's work. In all these achievements, Daniel Hale Williams's memory lives.

Chronology

January 18, 1856	Daniel Hale Williams born in Hollidaysburg, Pennsylvania
1877	graduates from Classical Academy in Janesville, Wisconsin
1880	enrolls in Chicago Medical College
March 1883	receives M.D. degree from Chicago Medical College
1889	is appointed to Illinois Board of Health
December 1890	decides to found an interracial hospital and school for black nurses
May 4, 1891	Provident Hospital and Training School opens in Chicago
July 9, 1893	Williams performs first successful operation on the heart
September 1894	becomes chief surgeon of Freedmen's Hospital in Washington, D.C.
December 1895	Williams and others establish the National Medical Association, a medical society for black doctors
February 1898	Williams resigns from Freedmen's Hospital post
April 2, 1898	marries Alice Johnson
June 1898	is accused of bad management at Freedmen's
1902	sutures an injured spleen
1912	is made associate attending surgeon at St. Luke's Hospital and forced to resign from Provident
1913	becomes only black charter member of American College of Surgeons
1920	retires and moves to Idlewild, Michigan
August 4, 1931	Williams dies

Further Reading

Buckler, Helen. *Daniel Hale Williams: Negro Surgeon*. New York: Pitman Publishing Corp., 1968. The primary adult biography of Williams.

Comroe, Julius H., Jr. "Doctor, You Have Six Minutes." *Science 84*, January-February 1984. Describes the development of the heart-lung machine.

Haber, Louis. *Black Pioneers of Science and Invention*. New York: Harcourt, Brace & World, 1970. For young adults. Devotes a chapter to Williams.

Hayden, Robert C. *Seven Black American Scientists*. Reading, Pa.: Addison-Wesley, 1970. For young adults. Devotes a chapter to Williams. Not quite as detailed as Haber's chapter.

Logan, Rayford W., and Michael R. Winston, eds., *Dictionary of American Negro Biography*. New York: Norton, 1982. Brief factual account of Williams's life and work.

"Moses of Negro Medicine." *Ebony*, February 1955. Detailed, well-illustrated article about Williams's life and work.

Riedman, Sarah R. *Masters of the Scalpel*. Chicago: Rand McNally, 1964. Provides background on the history of surgery, including development of antiseptic surgery.

Tuesday magazine, *Black Heroes in World History*. New York: Bantam, 1969. For young adults. Devotes a chapter to Williams.

George Washington Carver
(c.1865–1943)

*George Washington Carver. Carver gave
up studies in pure science to seek ways
to help poor southern farmers
improve their lives.*
(Courtesy Tuskegee University Archives.)

*I*n a deserted quarry in Kenya, where the only soil used to be the barren white powder of fossil coral, a farm is thriving. Trees surrounding the farm provide shade, firewood, and poles for building. They also hold the topsoil in place, thus preventing erosion, and add nutrients to the soil. Grass grows in the thin layer of soil made by the trees' leaf litter. The farm's sheep, goats, and a few cattle eat the grass and in turn provide meat and fertilizer. This productive farm uses only materials that the poorest farmer would have.

In a different part of Africa, a tribe of small, forest-dwelling people called the Efe begin to grow a new farm crop. It is a plant called the winged bean that originally came from Southeast Asia.

Like the trees around the quarry farm, the winged bean adds nutrients to the soil. Different parts of the plant, furthermore, can be used to make a variety of foods. The winged bean plants provide enough vitamins, protein, starches, and oil to meet most of the Efe's nutritional needs.

Ninety percent of new cars made in Brazil today run on alcohol fuel rather than gasoline. The fuel is made from parts of sugarcane, cassava, and other farm crops that used to be regarded as waste. Because the Brazilians turn these waste products into fuel, they need to import very little gasoline.

The people involved in these projects may never have heard of a black American called George Washington Carver. If Carver could visit the projects, however, he would probably understand the thinking behind them perfectly. Carver tried to use these same kinds of ideas among poor farmers in the American South almost a hundred years ago.

Like many blacks born into slavery, George Washington Carver was not sure of his birth date. It was some time during the Civil War (1861–65). His mother, Mary, was the one adult slave belonging to Moses and Susan Carver, a couple who owned a prosperous farm in Diamond (or Diamond Grove), Missouri. George Carver's father, a slave on a nearby farm, was killed in an accident soon after George was born.

Although Moses Carver owned a slave, he didn't like slavery, and he supported the Union during the war. This made him unpopular with some people in his part of southwestern Missouri, near the border of slaveholding Arkansas. One night border raiders attacked the Carver farm, kidnapped Mary and baby George, and took them into Arkansas. Moses Carver did his best to get them back. Mary was never seen again, but a neighbor at last brought George, seriously ill with whooping cough, back to the Carver household. Carver rewarded the man by giving him a horse.

Moses and Susan Carver, who had no children, raised George and his older half-brother, Jim, almost as if the boys were part of their own family. George and Jim lived in the Carvers' cabin with them. As the two boys grew older, Jim helped with the farm work, but George, who remained sickly, was given easier jobs. He usually helped Susan with cooking, sewing, laundry, and other household chores. In his free time he wandered outside. "I wanted to know the name of every stone and flower and insect and bird and beast," Carver wrote later. "I wanted to know where it got its color, where it got its life—but there was no one to tell me." The Carvers taught him to read and write a little, using an old spelling book.

George quickly learned that getting an education was not easy for a black. He and Jim played with white children from nearby farms and even went to Sunday school with them, but the two black boys were not allowed to attend the regular school in Diamond. When George learned that there was a school for black children in Neosho, eight miles away, he asked the Carvers' permission to move there, even though he was only about 10 years old. Understanding his hunger for education, the Carvers agreed.

After a short time in the Neosho school, George realized that the teacher knew little more than he did, so he joined a wagon train going to Fort Scott, Kansas. During his teenage years he wandered from one town to another. He even lived for a few years on the Kansas frontier, homesteading in a sod house.

Carver, who kept the name of the only "parents" he had ever really known, finished high school in Minneapolis, Kansas. He then applied by mail to a small college in Highland, Kansas. He was accepted, only to be refused entrance when he arrived and the principal discovered that he was black.

In 1890 Carver entered Simpson College in Indianola, Iowa. At first he studied art—he loved to paint flowers—but art offered him little opportunity to earn a living. It also gave him little chance to help "his people." Carver therefore turned his love of living things toward science: the study of plants (botany) and farming (agriculture).

Carver gained his scientific education at Iowa State College in Ames, which he entered in 1891. Iowa State was well known as a center for agricultural research and education. Carver impressed his professors so much that they appointed him to the college's faculty as soon as he had completed his undergraduate work in 1894. He was Iowa State's first black faculty member.

During his years at Iowa State, Carver specialized in mycology, the study of the plantlike living things called fungi. Carver collected many kinds of fungi, especially those that caused plant diseases. L.H. Pammel, the mycology expert under whom he studied, later called Carver "the best collector I ever had in the department or have ever known." Some of the fungi Carver collected were new to science and were named after him.

George Washington Carver

In the spring of 1896, just as Carver was finishing the work needed to obtain his master of science degree in agriculture, he received a letter from Booker T. Washington. Washington had made Tuskegee Institute in Alabama, of which he was the principal, one of the best-known colleges offering vocational and teacher training for blacks. He asked Carver to head Tuskegee's new agricultural department and experiment station. "I cannot offer you money, position, or fame," Washington wrote. "The first two you have; the last, from the place you now occupy, you will no doubt achieve. These things I now ask you to give up. I offer you in their place work—hard, hard work—the task of bringing a people from degradation, poverty, and waste to full manhood."

"It has always been the one ideal of my life to be of the greatest good to the greatest number of 'my people' possible," Carver replied to Washington. He agreed to come to Tuskegee as soon as he had obtained his degree.

Carver arrived in Tuskegee in October 1896. Not everyone welcomed him. Some faculty members were jealous of Carver's advanced degree and the relatively high salary Washington had offered him. Carver, for his part, soon showed that he did not like taking orders, even from Booker T. Washington. Although these two strong-willed men respected each other greatly, they continued to argue until Washington's death almost 20 years later. Carver complained that Washington gave him too many different jobs to do and offered too little support. Washington, in turn, scolded Carver because Carver was not a good administrator. Washington did, however, recognize Carver's strengths. He concluded a highly critical letter by acknowledging, "You are a great teacher, a great lecturer, a great inspirer of young men. . . . You also have great ability in original research."

Washington had warned Carver that he would find conditions at Tuskegee very different from those at Iowa State: "Your department exists only on paper, . . . and your laboratory will have to be in your head." Carver indeed discovered that if he wanted a laboratory, he would have to build it himself. "I went to the a trash pile at Tuskegee Institute," he remembered later, "and started my laboratory with bottles, old fruit jars and any other thing I found I could use." His first experiments were "worked out almost wholly on top of my flat topped writing desk and with teacups, glasses, bottles and reagents I made myself."

Like the scientists in the much better equipped agricultural laboratories of colleges such as Iowa State, Carver tried to use the

Carver as an old man in his laboratory. Carver set up his first laboratory with supplies he found in a trash pile at Tuskegee Institute.
(Courtesy Tuskegee University Archives.)

techniques of science to help farmers. For example, he analyzed soil samples sent in by farmers and told them which nutrients needed to be added to the soil. Most laboratories devoted to "scientific agriculture," however, looked for ways to use technology, such as new machines and artificial fertilizers, to grow crops more efficiently on large farms. Carver, by contrast, wanted to help "the man farthest down," the poor farmer. He knew that such farmers could neither understand nor afford new technology. Science needed to aid them in other ways.

Carver believed that most farmers in the South, both white and black, remained poor for several reasons. First, they depended on a single cash crop—cotton. Cotton drew nutrients out of the soil until the soil was worn out. When poor soil produced a meager crop, farmers abandoned their land and cleared more, cutting down forests and leaving soil open to destructive erosion. Attacks by an insect pest called the boll weevil made dependence on cotton even more dangerous.

Carver used his laboratory and Tuskegee's 10 acres of experiment station land to test crops other than cotton that might be grown in southern soil. The most useful ones, he decided, were cowpeas, peanuts, and sweet potatoes. Pod-bearing plants such as peanuts and cowpeas are called legumes. Their roots are swollen with lumps, or nodules, that contain bacteria. The bacteria can change nitrogen gas in the air into nitrites, which are essential nutrients for plants. Legumes, therefore, add nutrients to the soil. Carver knew that if farmers alternated crops of legumes with cotton, the legumes would add to the soil what the cotton took away. Sweet potatoes didn't add nutrients to the soil, but they used up few nutrients and grew well in poor soil.

These three crops could also help to solve another of the poor farmers' problems, malnutrition. By Carver's time, scientists had learned that many farmers accused of being lazy were in fact sick because of a lack of vitamins and protein in their diets. Carver showed that peanuts, sweet potatoes, and cowpeas had high nutritional value. In fact, he claimed that a diet consisting only of peanuts and sweet potatoes could provide all the nutrients that a human being needed. In his simple laboratory he used "cookstove chemistry" to work out new recipes that used these foods.

Carver also used his laboratory to help farmers fight economic dependence, a third problem that kept them poor. Most of these farmers either rented or worked on land owned by richer people, from whom they had to buy all their seeds, tools, and other farming supplies. They almost always owed more money than they could earn from their crops, so they remained tied to the land. Everything they bought pushed them deeper into debt. Carver therefore looked for ways that farmers could get things they needed from natural materials rather than by buying them. For example, he urged farmers to use leaves, garbage, swamp mud, and animal manure instead of commercial fertilizer. He found ways for farmers to make paints and dyes from the clay soil around Tuskegee.

Increased demand for southern farmers' crops would also help poor farmers become more independent. Knowing this, Carver broke down peanut plants and other farm products into their component parts in his laboratory and experimented with making both foods and industrial products from them. He even tried to find uses for materials, such as peanut shells, that most people threw away. Carver believed strongly that nature produced no waste; everything had a use that was merely waiting to be discovered. "TAKE CARE OF THE WASTE OF THE FARM AND TURN IT INTO USEFUL CHANNELS should be the slogan of every farmer," he once wrote.

Carver (second from right) with some of his students. Booker T. Washington described Carver as "a great teacher" and "a great inspirer of young men."
(Courtesy Library of Congress.)

Carver and Booker Washington agreed that getting these new ideas to the farmers who needed them was the hardest part of their educational task. They started several programs that brought farmers to Tuskegee, but they wanted to reach farmers who remained in the countryside as well. For farmers who could read, Carver published bulletins or articles that offered practical farming advice in simple language. To reach farmers who could not read, Carver and Washington designed "movable schools": wagons containing farming equipment, exhibits and charts that could be taken into the countryside by "demonstration agents" who would explain the ideas behind the exhibits. The movable schools were so successful that the U.S. Department of Agriculture soon made such wagons part of their general program to help farmers.

Carver was an inspiring teacher, whether his audience was farmers in the Alabama countryside, students in a Tuskegee classroom, or, later, listeners in auditoriums across the country. He impressed people partly because of his unusual teaching approach. Instead of presenting traditional courses in botany, meteorology (the study of weather), entomology (the study of insects), and so on, Carver had his students study a single kind of plant in detail. They learned how all the forces of nature affected that one plant. In this way they came to share Carver's vision of all of nature, and all of the sciences that studied nature, as parts of a whole. To Carver, the main purpose of education was "understanding relationships."

Carver also inspired his students by his obvious love of his subject and his personal warmth. Students found that he was interested in their lives as well as their studies. Later in his life, Carver extended this warmth to students he met during his many trips to other college campuses. White or black, these students became "his children"—the only children he had, since he never married. He exchanged loving letters with many of them all his life.

Carver's life at Tuskegee changed after 1915, when Booker T. Washington died. Carver was by then in his fifties. Robert Moton, Tuskegee's new principal, gave Carver more freedom to travel instead of teach.

As Carver gave lectures and showed exhibits of the products he had discovered, his fame began to grow. In 1916 he was made a member of Britain's Royal Society of the Arts. When World War I brought shortages of certain imported goods, federal officials consulted Carver about some of his products, such as rubber from sweet potatoes and dyes from clays. The war ended, however, before any of his suggestions could be put into production.

Peanuts brought Carver his greatest fame. Increasing numbers of farmers in the South had begun growing peanuts even before Carver started to talk about the many things that could be made from them. Peanut growers often had trouble finding a market for their crop, however. They hoped that Carver, with his dramatic speaking style and unusual range of peanut products, would change that if he became their spokesperson.

Carver proved the peanut growers right when he spoke on their behalf at a hearing of the House of Representatives' Ways and Means Committee in 1921. The committee was meeting to decide which products would be included in a proposed tariff, or tax, on imported goods. The tariff was supposed to protect key American products by raising the price of foreign goods that might compete with them. To have peanuts included in the tariff, Carver had to convince the committee that peanuts were valuable to the country.

Carver was given only 10 minutes to make his speech. When he started, he was greeted with laughter and racist remarks. As he pulled more and more samples from his battered suitcase, however, the committee's interest grew. Carver displayed several breakfast foods, an abrasive powder that could be used to polish tin, a variety of candies and sweets, foods for livestock, flour and meal, "milk," many shades of dye, and much more—all made from peanuts. Again and again, the committee chairperson extended Carver's speaking time. When Carver finished, the committee members voted to include peanuts in the tariff.

White southern leaders were among those who praised Carver's products. Most of the South in the 1920s and 1930s depended on agriculture. Since prices for farm goods were very poor in those years, the area was poverty stricken. The southern leaders hoped to replace farming with industry and thereby create an economic resurgence that would lead to a "New South." Most had little regard for black people, but they hoped that some of Carver's inventions would further their aims. Carver was willing to work with these leaders because he shared their love of the land and their belief in the South's potential for economic growth.

Although Carver apparently was not interested in making money for himself (he often did not even bother to cash his salary checks from Tuskegee), he did seek patents for some of his products and was awarded three. He also took part in a few commercial ventures, including attempts to sell paint products made from Alabama clays and medicines made from peanut oil. None of these ventures was successful.

Carver nonetheless became more and more famous. Awed by the more than 300 products he claimed to have made from the peanut alone, people began calling him "the Peanut Man" and "The Wizard of Tuskegee." Journalists wrote article after article about him, lavishing him with praise. He was hailed as a pioneer in the new applied science of chemurgy, or the finding of industrial uses for agricultural products. Foreign governments sought his advice (his peanut milk was used in Africa, for example), and influential men such as Henry Ford became his admirers and friends. All kinds of groups deluged him with awards. The National Association for the Advancement of Colored People (NAACP) awarded him its Spingarn Medal in 1923. In 1939 he was given the Roosevelt Medal for distinguished service, and the Thomas A. Edison Foundation gave him an award in 1943.

By the late 1930s Carver was in his seventies, and his health began to fail. He wanted to make sure that his life and ideas would not be forgotten. He therefore gave his life's savings—a surprisingly large amount, thanks apparently to the fact that he had saved almost all of what he had earned—to create a museum devoted to his life and a foundation that would support young black scientists who wanted to carry on his work. Once Carver's plans became known, people all over the country sent donations to help him.

The George Washington Carver Foundation was established in 1940. Today it is a highly respected research center. Carver's museum, finished in 1941, showed not only his products made from peanuts, sweet potatoes, and so on but also 71 of his paintings (many made with natural dyes) and even knitting and other needlework that he had done. Carver saw all these activities as part of a single effort, "seeking Truth."

Carver died on January 5, 1943, when he was about 80 years old. He was buried at Tuskegee, next to Booker T. Washington. At his funeral President Franklin D. Roosevelt said, "The world of science has lost one of its most eminent figures. . . . The versatility of his genius and his achievements in . . . the arts and sciences were truly amazing." A few months after his death the federal government made his birthplace a national monument. It was the first national monument to honor a black. Carver has been given many other awards in the years after his death.

Few American scientists of any race have become as well known, admired, and beloved as George Washington Carver. Carver once wrote that "When you can do the common things of life in an uncommon way you'll command the attention of the world," and nothing demonstrated the truth of this statement more perfectly than his own life.

Carver became famous partly because his personality apparently made most of those who met him become his admirers and friends. He also gained more public acclaim than most scientists because his discoveries promised to be useful in everyday life and he described them in terms that everyone could understand. Most important, perhaps, his life was a romantic success story that appealed to many people. A variety of groups used that story for their own purposes, and Carver seldom seems to have stopped them. When journalists made exaggerated claims about his achievements, he corrected them only with general statements such as "I do not deserve all the credit you have given me." Such statements were taken merely as signs of modesty, and the exaggerated stories continued to spread.

Some scientists have felt that Carver's fame was at least partly undeserved. Although Carver's religious beliefs inspired some people, they angered others who saw religion and science as having nothing in common. "No books ever go into my laboratory," Carver said in a speech in 1924. Instead, he claimed, he spoke directly to "Mr. Creator" and was inspired to do whatever was needed. The next day a *New York Times* reporter wrote an angry editorial about the speech, titled "Men of Science Never Talk That Way." It accused Carver of "a complete lack of the scientific spirit."

Scientists and historians critical of Carver have pointed out that he seldom wrote down the formulas and procedures that he used in making his products. This made it hard for other scientists to duplicate his work, and such duplication is an important part of the testing of scientific ideas. Furthermore, these critics have noted, many of the products that Carver exhibited were not really his own inventions; they had been in general use before he displayed them. (This was one reason why he gained so few patents.) Some of the products also were very similar to each other. Thus, the number of products that Carver claimed to have invented seems to have been exaggerated. The products also were not commercially successful. In short, critics of Carver's reputation have claimed that Carver made few, if any, significant discoveries in either pure or applied science.

As Linda McMurry, a recent biographer of Carver, has pointed out, Carver's most important contributions to science may be ideas that were not fully appreciated during his life. Today ecology, the study of the relationships between living things and their environment, teaches just as Carver did that living and nonliving things in nature interact as parts of a whole. Ideas proposed by Carver, such as using legumes as soil enrichers and food crops, are being applied successfully in Third World countries (where the winged bean is being grown, for example). Scientists are working, just as Carver did, to find uses for waste products, such as making auto fuel from them. They also are trying to find ways to fertilize land and control pests by using natural, or organic, materials rather than wasteful and sometimes dangerous synthetic chemicals.

These modern achievements did not grow directly out of George Washington Carver's work, nor was he the first to express the ideas behind them. Nonetheless, he did his best to spread these ideas at a time when few other scientists understood them. He brought them to the public's attention in impressive and dramatic ways. In doing so he was ahead of his time.

Chronology

c. 1865	George Washington Carver born in Diamond, Missouri
c. 1875	leaves Diamond to seek education
1890	enters Simpson College in Indianola, Iowa
1891	enters Iowa State College in Ames
1894	completes undergraduate training and joins faculty of Iowa State College
1896	gains master of science degree from Iowa State and joins faculty of Tuskegee Institute
1915	Booker T. Washington dies
1916	Carver made a member of Britain's Royal Society of the Arts
1921	gives lecture on uses of peanuts to House of Representatives' Ways and Means Committee
1923	is awarded Spingarn Medal by National Association for the Advancement of Colored People
1939	is awarded Roosevelt Medal for distinguished service
1940	George Washington Carver Foundation established
1941	George Washington Carver Museum opens
January 5, 1943	Carver dies
1943	Carver birthplace made a national monument

Further Reading

Adair, Gene. *George Washington Carver: Botanist.* New York: Chelsea House, 1989. A full-length biography written for young adults.

"Another Honor for the 'Peanut' Man." *Ebony*, July 1977. Article on Carver's life written on the occasion of his induction into the Hall of Fame for Great Americans.

Carver, George W. "Many Food Products Can Be Made from Peanut and Sweet Potato." *American Food Journal*, August 1921. Carver's short account of the nutritional value and many uses of these plants.

Haber, Louis. *Black Pioneers of Science and Invention.* New York: Harcourt, Brace & World, 1970. For young adults. Chapter is favorable to Carver.

Hayden, Robert C. *Seven Black American Scientists.* Reading, Pa.: Addison-Wesley, 1970. For young adults. Chapter is favorable to Carver.

Kremer, Gary R. *George Washington Carver in His Own Words.* Columbia: University of Missouri Press, 1987. Quotes extensively from Carver's letters and other writings to illuminate his life.

Logan, Rayford W., and Michael R. Winston, eds. *Dictionary of American Negro Biography.* New York: Norton, 1982. Provides a short factual sketch of Carver's life and work.

Mackintosh, Barry. "George Washington Carver and the Peanut." *American Heritage*, August 1977. Attempts to separate facts from myths about Carver's life; critical of Carver.

McMurry, Linda O. *George Washington Carver: Scientist and Symbol.* New York: Oxford University Press, 1981. Probably the most factual and carefully researched adult biography of Carver; provides a balanced view of his achievements.

Ernest Everett Just
(1883–1941)

*Ernest Everett Just. Just examined cells carefully
under a microscope to learn how they worked.*
(Courtesy Moorland-Spingarn Research Center,
Howard University.)

A cell—the basic unit of which almost all living things are made—
floats in liquid. Like most cells, it contains an inner structure
called a nucleus. Inside the nucleus lie coiled molecules, divided
into units called genes, that carry information inherited from the
cell's parent organisms. Around the nucleus, living matter called
cytoplasm pulses and quivers. The cell is enclosed by a membrane
that separates it from the liquid outside it.

Now a group of smaller cells swims toward the first, large one.
Each of these small cells looks like a tadpole, with a bulging head
attached to a wildly flailing tail. The first swimming cell to reach

the large cell rams into the large cell's membrane. The large cell's surface quivers, as if from the impact. Then suddenly the swimming cell's head is buried in the larger cell's membrane. Starting from this point of entry, chemical changes sweep like a wave around the rim of the larger cell. No other swimming cells will be able to enter the large cell after the progress of the wave is complete.

This scene is the first act in a drama that is perhaps the most important in all biology: the beginning of a new life. The large cell is an egg cell, the reproductive cell of a female organism. The swimming cells are sperm cells, which come from the male. The process during which an egg and a sperm unite is called fertilization. After this process is complete, the fertilized egg cell will divide and divide again, finally developing into a new organism.

Black scientist Ernest Everett Just spent his life trying to understand this central mystery of biology. Working painstakingly with the eggs and sperm of simple sea animals, he discovered new facts about fertilization and pointed the way toward a better understanding of the way all cells work.

Charleston, South Carolina, had just finished celebrating the centennial of its incorporation as a city when Ernest Everett Just was born there on August 14, 1883. Charles Fraser Just, Ernest Just's father, and Charles Just, Sr., his grandfather, were wharf builders. His father and grandfather both died, however, when Ernest was only four.

Ernest's mother, Mary Matthews Just, had to support herself, Ernest, and his younger brother and sister. For a while she spent part of each year teaching school in Charleston and part working in the phosphate quarry on nearby James Island (phosphate was used in commercial fertilizer). She saved enough money to buy some land on the island and organize a small community, which was called Maryville in her honor. It had one of the first entirely black town governments in the state. Mary Just took special charge of education in Maryville and eventually spent all her time teaching there.

Ernest learned what he could from his mother. Then, at age 13, he entered South Carolina State College in Orangeburg, a sort of elementary and vocational school for blacks. He attended this school for three years.

Mary Just encouraged Ernest to go north to seek a better education. In 1900 he enrolled in Kimball Union Academy, a college-preparatory high school in Meriden, New Hampshire. At the time he began studying there, Ernest Just was the only black on campus. In addition to doing excellent academic work, he took part in plays, the debating society, and the school newspaper.

Just enrolled at Dartmouth, a highly respected college in Hanover, New Hampshire, in 1903. At first he continued the studies in Greek and Latin that he had begun at Kimball. In his sophomore year, however, he took a course called "The Principles of Biology" that fascinated him. He soon changed his major to biology. Just was a Rufus Choate Scholar, the highest academic award for an undergraduate at Dartmouth, in his junior and senior years. He also was elected to Phi Beta Kappa, the academic honor society. He was the only student in his class to graduate *magna cum laude* (with great praise).

Upon his graduation in 1907, Just faced the same problem as all other black college graduates of his time: No matter how brilliant they were or how high their grades, it was almost impossible for blacks to become faculty members of white colleges or universities. Just therefore took what seemed the best of the choices available to him and joined the faculty of Howard University in Washington, D.C. Howard was one of the best black universities. It boasted a highly regarded medical school, which owed some of its quality to improvements made by Daniel Hale Williams in the training of doctors at the university's associated Freedmen's Hospital. When Howard opened a new science building in 1910, the college's president, Wilbur P. Thirkield, put Just in charge of the biology department. A separate department in zoology, or the study of animals, was established two years later, with Just at its head.

Just enjoyed teaching and helping students. In addition to working with students in the classroom, he started Howard's first drama club and helped to organize Omega Psi Phi, a national all-black fraternity. His first love, however, was always research. He asked his Dartmouth biology professor, William Patten, to help him find a place where he could take graduate training in zoology. Patten introduced him to Frank R. Lillie, head of the Department of Zoology at the University of Chicago. Lillie also was the director of the Marine Biological Laboratory (MBL) at Woods Hole, Massachusetts. Then, as now, many of the world's best biologists spent their summers at the MBL, studying the fascinating organisms that thronged the ocean off Woods Hole during warm weather.

Lillie warned Just that graduate training would not improve his job prospects and might simply make him more frustrated. Lillie agreed to accept Just as his laboratory assistant, however, and count the work Just did at the MBL as credit toward completion of a Ph.D. degree with the University of Chicago. Just spent his first summer in Woods Hole in 1909, and he was there every summer except one thereafter for the next 20 years.

As graduate students usually do, Just assisted his professor in his research and at the same time began projects of his own. Just and Lillie became close friends and remained so throughout Just's life. Following Lillie's lead, Just did research on the fertilization process in the eggs of simple marine animals such as sandworms, sand dollars, and sea urchins. These animals release egg and sperm cells into the water in huge quantities, which makes the cells easy to collect and study.

Just's first research paper was published in 1912. He showed that the point at which a sperm cell enters the egg cell (which can be anywhere on the cell) determines the location of the plane along which the fertilized egg will begin to divide. In other words, the

Sea urchins. Ernest Everett Just studied the eggs of these and other simple sea animals to learn about the process through which life begins.
(Courtesy Marty Snyderman.)

interaction between the egg cell's surface and its environment (the sperm) plays an important part in development. Fertilization, development, and the role of the cell surface continued to be Just's greatest interests for the rest of his life.

Teaching at Howard and experimenting at Woods Hole did not take up all of Just's time. On June 26, 1912, he married Ethel Highwarden, who taught German at Howard. As time went on they had three children, Margaret, Highwarden, and Maribel. Ethel Just did not share her husband's interest in science. She usually remained in their comfortable home in Washington with the children when Just traveled to do his research.

An important part of Just's work life, like that of the other scientists at Woods Hole, was collecting the sea animals on which experiments were to be performed. Just and other scientists went down to the shore or out on the MBL's two collecting boats at all hours to get fresh specimens. Their collecting nets brought up an assortment of squid, fish, snails, and other marine creatures. These had to be sorted and identified before being taken back to the lab.

One of the animals that Just found most interesting to collect was the sandworm, *Nereis*. These small worms swarmed to the surface of the water in great numbers during their breeding season. Almost every evening during the summers of 1911, 1912, and 1913 Just went out with a lantern and some collecting dishes and lay on a float in the pond behind the MBL supply building. After sunset but before moonrise the tiny male worms appeared. Colored a brilliant red, they swam through the water in curving paths. Then a smaller number of large, slow-moving, yellow-green female worms swam up to join the males. Just watched by the light of his lantern as the males shed their sperm in clouds that turned the water milky. Then the females released their eggs and sank down through the water to die. Together with Lillie, Just wrote an article on the breeding habits of *Nereis* that was published in 1913.

In 1912 at Woods Hole, Just met Jacques Loeb, a famous biologist who worked at the Rockefeller Institute for Medical Research. Loeb admired both Just's research and his teaching at Howard. When the National Association for the Advancement of Colored People (NAACP) decided to award a medal, called the Spingarn Medal, each year to "the man or woman of African descent who shall have made the highest achievement during the preceding year, or years, in any honorable field of human endeavor," Loeb nominated Just for the award. Although Just was not well known to the public, Loeb pointed out, he was a respected scientist, and giving him the medal would help to counteract the belief that blacks could not achieve in highly intellectual subjects such as science. Just received the first Spingarn Medal on February 12, 1915. Later other black scientists, including George Washington Carver, Percy Julian, and Charles Drew, also received this award.

The Spingarn Medal won national headlines for Just and his work. Recognition by the scientific community, however, was much more important to him. Just knew he needed to get his Ph.D. degree in order to continue his scientific career. He spent the 1915–16 academic year at the University of Chicago taking classes that, along with the work he had done at Woods Hole, would fulfill the requirements for the degree. He received his Ph.D. in June 1916, becoming one of only a handful of blacks who had gained this degree from a major university.

Just paid more attention than most of the Woods Hole scientists to the breeding habits of the sea creatures he studied and the exact conditions under which their eggs normally developed. A good part of the fame he won as a research scientist over the years, in fact, came from his careful observation and patient laboratory work. Frank Lillie wrote that Just knew sea animals and their eggs better "than probably any other person." Many scientists at Woods Hole, experienced as well as new ones, consulted Just about the best ways to care for marine specimens. Eventually he wrote a series of articles for the Woods Hole newspaper, *The Collecting Net*, that described his methods in detail. These articles were reprinted in 1939 as a short book, *Basic Methods for Experiments on Eggs of Marine Animals*.

Just continued to teach at Howard, but his heart was not in this work. Although he felt some duty to improve black education, he was always more of a research scientist than a teacher, and research, at that time, was all but impossible at Howard. Like most black colleges and universities, Howard had almost no money to spend on laboratory equipment and buildings. Most people at the school, furthermore, had little understanding of or interest in pure research. "I have always felt out of place at Howard," Just wrote late in his life. He called it "a make-believe university." Trying to keep Just at Howard was, fellow researcher Benjamin Karpman wrote, "like putting an eagle in a chicken coop." Because Just was black, however, there seemed to be no better place that he could go.

Just's salary from Howard was not enough to finance his research work. He therefore sought financial grants from philanthropic foundations. Many scientists do this today, but the practice was less common in Just's time, especially for a black person. In fact, no black scientist before Just had received foundation support for research in pure science.

During the 1920s Just received several major grants from a fund set up by Julius Rosenwald, who had made a fortune through the Sears, Roebuck mail-order business. The grants allowed Just to spend only half of each year teaching at Howard, leaving him free to spend the other half doing research. Just also received grants from the National Research Council, the General Education Board, the Carnegie Corporation, and others. These grants showed the high regard in which his work was held. Each grant covered only a short period, however, so Just never had the financial security that would have come from a permanent place on the faculty of a large university.

By 1929 Just felt that he had gone as far as he could go, both personally and professionally, not only at Howard but at Woods Hole. His eyes turned toward Europe. His work was well known among scientists there. In fact, it was better known in Europe than in the United States, partly because more European scientists were interested in the kind of research he was doing. He had been invited to speak at European conferences and to serve as an editor on European scientific journals. Just believed that European scientists would respect him and treat him as an equal in a way that American scientists, even those at Woods Hole, sometimes did not. Furthermore, working at European laboratories would allow him to do research on animals similar to but different from those he had studied at Woods Hole. Showing that his experimental findings applied to a variety of animals would increase the usefulness and importance of his work.

Just went to Europe for the first time in January 1929. He worked at the Zoological Station in Naples, Italy, a laboratory much like the MBL. He felt at home there immediately. He was equally happy the following year when he spent six months as a visiting professor at the Kaiser Wilhelm Institute in Berlin, Germany. It was a great honor to be asked to go to this famous research laboratory, which included several Nobel Prize winners on its staff. No American had been invited there before.

Ernest Everett Just

Just cut short his stay in Germany in order to return to Woods Hole in June 1930 for a 60th birthday party given for his old friend and teacher, Frank Lillie. However, he told people during the party that "I have received more in the way of fraternity and assistance in my one year at the Kaiser Wilhelm Institute than in all my other years at Woods Hole put together." He never went back to the MBL.

In Europe Just broadened the focus of his work. His studies of developing eggs led him to believe that the cell surface and the part of the cell material, or cytoplasm, that lay just under the surface played a very important part in the cell's activities. Most other scientists had paid little attention to these parts of the cell. Some were not even sure that the cell membrane existed.

Just summarized his ideas in a book, *The Biology of the Cell Surface*, which was published in 1939. The book explained the special significance of the outer cytoplasm, which Just called the ectoplasm.

> As the boundary, the living mobile limit of the cell, the ectoplasm controls the integration between the living cell and all else external to it. . . . It stands guard over the peculiar form of the living substance, is buffer against the attacks of the surroundings and the means of communication with it.

Just's earlier work had proven that the ectoplasm was necessary for fertilization and normal development. He also showed that the cell surface was involved in important phenomena such as conduction of nerve impulses and contraction of muscle cells. He came to believe that the ectoplasm was more important than the genes in the nucleus in carrying hereditary information. "Only in as much as they take out substances from the cytoplasm do the genes determine heredity," he said.

Just's book presented not only a new theory about the importance of the cell surface but a new philosophy of biology. He proposed a middle path between the two points of view common among biologists of his time, those of the "mechanists" and those of the "vitalists." The mechanists believed that a complete understanding of living things could be obtained by breaking them down into their component molecules and atoms and studying them by the methods of physics and chemistry, exactly as nonliving things were studied. The vitalists held that living things possessed an unidentifiable, mystical "something" that could never be studied by such means.Nothing in living things contradicts physics and chemistry, Just said. Physics and chemistry alone cannot explain how living things work, however, because living things possess a degree of organization that is not present in separate atoms and molecules. "Living substance is such because it possesses this organization—something more than the sum of its minutest parts," he wrote. "Life is exquisitely a time-thing like music." In order to understand the organization that makes life possible, Just emphasized, scientists had to study whole cells and organisms under normal conditions.

Furthermore, Just saw the organization of the cell as a miniature mirror of the organization and the interrelatedness of all nature. "We feel the beauty of Nature because we are part of Nature and because we know that however much in our separate domains we abstract from the unity of Nature, this unity remains," Just wrote at the end of his book. "So in our study of the animal egg: though we resolve it into constituent parts the better to understand it, we hold it as an integrated thing, as a unified system."

In the 1930s Just continued to teach at Howard and spend his summers doing research in Europe. Although he was happiest in Europe, his life there often was not easy. Grants were very hard to get during the economic depression of the 1930s, so Just seldom had much money. Furthermore, political changes in Europe made it harder and harder to work there. In 1933 an extremist group led by Adolf Hitler, the National Socialists, or Nazis, took control of Germany. The Nazis did not welcome foreigners, and Just did not work in Germany after 1933. Instead, he did research in Italy and, later, France.

In poor health and exhausted by constant disagreements with the administration at Howard, Just decided in 1938 to move to France for good. The Sorbonne, France's great academic institution, allowed him to work at its marine research station in Roscoff, on the country's northwest coast. When Germany and France went to war near the end of 1939, however, the French government ordered all foreign scientists to leave the country. Unable to escape before Paris fell to the Germans, Just was captured and held briefly in a prisoner-of-war camp before finally being allowed to return to the United States in September 1940.

Just went back to Howard; he had nowhere else to go. Howard officials ordered him to return to teaching, but he was too ill. Just's increasingly severe digestive troubles proved to be due to cancer. He died on October 27, 1941.

Just's old teacher and friend, Frank Lillie, wrote of Just's scientific work, "He has been easily one of the most productive investigators at Woods Hole. . . . His studies have been characterized not only by their care and precision, but also by a very considerable degree of scientific imagination. I do not think that any qualified zoologist would maintain that his work was not strictly first class."

Other scientists, for the most part, have agreed. Benjamin Karpman wrote in the *Journal of Nervous and Mental Diseases*,

> *He was a most tireless and persistent worker whose quality of work will match the highest. The total number of his [written] contributions come to about sixty. . . . [They] were models of scientific presentation—succinct, precise, direct with economy of words. . . . His book,* The Biology of the Cell Surface, *which synthesizes his life work, is a remarkable contribution of highest scientific order.*

Charles Richard Drew, who was to follow in Just's footsteps as a researcher and teacher at Howard, said that Just was "a biologist of unusual skill and the greatest of our original thinkers in the field."

To be sure, time has proven some of Just's ideas wrong. The cytoplasm is not, as he believed, more important than the genes in carrying hereditary information. Many of the important functions that he attributed to the ectoplasm belong in fact to the cell membrane. Neither Just nor other scientists of his time could study this membrane in detail because it is almost invisible under an ordinary light microscope, and the electron microscope, which can show the cell membrane clearly, had not yet been invented.

Just was correct, however, in saying that the outer part of the cell was much more important than scientists had previously thought. He was also ahead of his time in stressing the importance of interactions among different parts of the cell and between the cell and its environment. He brought to science a new emphasis on the need to understand the normal behavior of cells and organisms and to make sure that experimental conditions did not distort that behavior unintentionally. Finally, like George Washington Carver, Just saw cells, living things, and nature itself as organized wholes made up of closely related parts. This view is a keystone of scientific thinking in biology today.

In spite of the national attention he gained when he was given the Spingarn Medal and some of the Rosenwald grants, Just never received the kind of popular acclaim given to George Washington Carver. Just did, however, win a sort of approval that, for the most part, Carver never gained and that Just valued much more highly: the admiration and respect of other scientists. Like a later black scientist, Bertram Fraser-Reid, Ernest Everett Just showed that a black person could do outstanding work in pure laboratory science and could make significant contributions toward human understanding of the basic nature of life.

Chronology

August 14, 1883	Ernest Everett Just born in Charleston, South Carolina
1900	enrolls in Kimball Union Academy
1903	enrolls at Dartmouth
1907	graduates from Dartmouth *magna cum laude*; joins faculty of Howard University
1909	spends first summer at Marine Biological Laboratory
1912	is made head of Howard's zoology department; has first research paper published
June 26, 1912	marries Ethel Highwarden
1913	Just's article on the breeding habits of the sandworm (*Nereis*) published
February 12, 1915	Just receives NAACP's first Spingarn Medal
June 1916	receives Ph.D. degree from University of Chicago
January 1929	does research in Europe for the first time
1930	becomes visiting professor at Kaiser Wilhelm Institute in Germany
1933	ceases to work in Germany after Nazis take control of the country
1938	decides to move to France permanently
1939	Just's books, *The Biology of the Cell Surface* and *Basic Methods for Experiments in Eggs of Marine Animals*, published
September 1940	Just returns to United States after being held briefly as a prisoner of war in France
October 27, 1941	Just dies

Further Reading

Gould, Stephen Jay. "Just in the Middle." *Natural History*, January 1984. Describes Just's position between the mechanists and the vitalists and evaluates his work as a whole.

Haber, Louis. *Black Pioneers of Science and Invention*. New York: Harcourt, Brace & World, 1970. For young adults. Devotes a chapter to Just.

Hayden, Robert C. *Seven Black American Scientists*. Reading, Mass.: Addison-Wesley, 1970. For young adults. Devotes a chapter to Just.

Just, Ernest E. *The Biology of the Cell Surface*. Philadelphia: Blakiston, 1939. Describes Just's theories about cell organization and the importance of the ectoplasm.

Lillie, Frank R. "Ernest Everett Just." *Science*, January 2, 1942. Obituary of Just written by his longtime friend and teacher.

Logan, Rayford W., and Michael R. Winston, eds., *Dictionary of American Negro Biography*. New York: Norton, 1982. Short factual review of Just's life and career.

Manning, Kenneth R. *Black Apollo of Science*. New York: Oxford University Press, 1983. The only full-length adult biography of Just; carefully researched.

Rogers, J.A. *World's Great Men of Color*, Volume II. New York: Collier Books, 1972. A chapter describes Just's life and work.

Percy Lavon Julian
(1899–1975)

Percy Lavon Julian. Julian, an organic chemist,
discovered ways to synthesize complex chemicals
important in industry and medicine.
(Courtesy Moorland-Springarn Research Center,
Howard University, and Associated Publishers.)

*F*ifty years ago, people with arthritis led miserable lives. Their joints
grew more swollen, inflamed, and deformed as the disease pro-
gressed. The simplest tasks, such as getting dressed, became agoniz-
ingly difficult. Moving around became harder and more painful
until, finally, many arthritis victims could not walk at all.

Then, in 1948, doctors at the famous Mayo Clinic in Rochester, Minnesota, discovered that cortisone could control the pain

and inflammation of arthritis. Cortisone is one of a group of natural body chemicals called hormones. When given repeated doses of cortisone as a drug, many arthritis sufferers once again became able to walk, use their hands, and lead normal lives. The treatment seemed like a miracle.

There was only one problem. Cortisone had to be made from animal products. Normally it is made in the outer parts of two small glands on top of the kidneys, called the adrenal glands. Scientists had to use tons of animal adrenal glands in the experiments that first identified the hormone in 1935. Doctors could not consider using cortisone as a medical treatment at that time because it was available only in such tiny amounts.

In 1946 scientists learned how to make cortisone from a digestive secretion called bile, taken from animals. That improved the supply enough for doctors to begin experimenting with the hormone. The process of making cortisone was still difficult, however, and the amount produced was very small. As a result, at the time cortisone's power as a "miracle" treatment for arthritis was discovered, the compound cost several hundred dollars a gram. A gram of hormone could treat a single arthritis patient for only 10 to 20 days. The bile of 14,600 oxen was needed to make enough cortisone to treat one patient for a year. The miracle thus was out of reach for all except the very rich.

A black chemist named Percy Lavon Julian changed that. Julian found ways to make cortisone cheaply from soybeans and yams, thus making the new arthritis treatment affordable for many more people. He also found inexpensive ways to make several other hormones and a drug used to treat a serious eye disease. He made industrial products from soybeans as well, including a lifesaving foam used to smother fires.

Percy Lavon Julian was born in Montgomery, Alabama, on April 11, 1899. He was the oldest of six children born to James and Margaret Julian. James Julian was a railway mail clerk. He insisted on excellence in everything his children did. One of Percy Julian's brothers remembered that one day young Percy got a score of 80 on a school test and brought the paper proudly to his father. James Julian told Percy sternly that 80 wasn't good enough: only 100, a perfect score, would do.

Percy Lavon Julian

Percy Julian became interested in chemistry while he was still a teenager. The black high school he attended had no chemistry classes, however. Indeed, it did not provide much education of any kind. When Julian entered DePauw University in Greencastle, Indiana, in 1916, he had to begin as a "subfreshman" and take makeup high school classes as well as college ones for his first two years. He also had to work to earn money for his tuition. He waited on tables in a white fraternity house and slept in the house's attic. In spite of this heavy schedule, he graduated at the top of his class in 1920. He was named the Phi Beta Kappa orator and the class valedictorian, or commencement speaker.

When Julian wanted to go to graduate school in chemistry, he encountered the same problem that Ernest Just had run into 17 years earlier: few graduate programs in science at major universities accepted black students, and none encouraged them. William Blanchard, one of Julian's professors at DePauw, tried to get him into good programs. Blanchard had to report to Julian, however, that he had been told, in effect, "I'd advise you to discourage your bright colored lad. We couldn't get him a job when he's done, and it'll only mean frustration. . . . Why don't you find him a teaching job in a Negro college in the South? He doesn't need a Ph.D. for that!"

Julian was bitterly disappointed, but he accepted what seemed to be unavoidable for the time being. He took a teaching position at Fisk, a respected black university in Nashville, Tennessee. He found that he liked teaching better than he had thought he would. His students inspired and challenged him so much that he completely rewrote his chemistry lecture notes. When he sent the new notes to Professor Blanchard at DePauw, Blanchard replied that he was going to tear up most of his own lecture notes and use Julian's instead.

After two years at Fisk, Julian won the Austin Fellowship, a graduate fellowship in chemistry that allowed him to attend prestigious Harvard University for a year. At the end of the 1922–23 academic year Julian emerged with a master's degree in chemistry, having made straight A's in all his classes. Normally a graduate student who did as well as Julian would have been made a teaching assistant after receiving his degree. Julian was not given this opportunity, however, because Harvard administrators feared that students from the South might refuse to be taught by a black man. Julian nonetheless remained at Harvard on "minor fellowships" until 1926.

Despairing of advancement in the white academic world, Julian returned to teaching in black colleges. He spent one year at the West Virginia State College for Negroes, where he was the entire chemistry department. In 1927 he joined the chemistry department at Howard University in Washington, D.C. Ernest Just was already the head of the zoology department there.

Like Just, Julian decided that he needed to continue his studies in Europe. Julian wanted to study under a famous Austrian chemist, Ernst Spaeth, who had synthesized (made artificially) several important natural chemicals. With the help of a grant from the General Education Board and some money from a rich Harvard friend, Julian set sail for Europe just six months after Just did—in June 1929.

Julian not only studied under Spaeth at the University of Vienna but lived in Spaeth's home and became his close friend, much as Just had become friends with Frank Lillie. From Spaeth Julian learned more about organic chemistry, or the chemistry of molecules that contain carbon. Organic chemistry includes the study of the many chemical compounds that make up the bodies of living things, though it is not limited to these compounds. Julian's particular interest, then and later, was in learning how simple organic compounds in plants and other natural materials could be combined to make the more complex compounds found in the human body. Among other things, Julian began to try to learn how certain sterols, or solid alcohols, that were related to important body chemicals could be made from soybeans. At that time soybeans grew mostly in Asia and had to be imported to Europe for research.

Julian received his Ph.D. degree from the University of Vienna in 1931. Unlike Just, he never planned to remain in Europe. Julian returned to Howard, where he was made the head of the chemistry department and had a chance to help plan a large new chemistry building. He also began trying to synthesize physostigmine, a drug important for the treatment of a serious eye disease called glaucoma.

In glaucoma, liquid accumulates inside the eye, making the pressure inside the eyeball rise. The high pressure damages the retina, the carpet of sensitive cells in the back of the eye that is necessary for vision, and thus eventually causes blindness. Physostigmine controls glaucoma by making the pupil (the black-looking opening in the front of the eye) contract. This allows liquid to flow out of the eye and thus lowers the pressure. Unfortunately, in the early 1930s physostigmine could be obtained only by extracting it from an African plant, the Calabar bean. If the drug could be made synthetically, a much larger supply of it would be available and it would become cheaper.

Like Ernest Just, Julian found research difficult at Howard. Julian especially missed trained assistants. He finally persuaded the Howard administration to let him hire two German men who had worked with him in Spaeth's laboratory. Julian's disagreements with Howard's administration continued, however, and he left the university in 1932.

Professor Blanchard, Julian's old friend, was now a dean at DePauw. He asked Julian to come back to the university, and Julian accepted. One of Julian's German assistants, Josef Pikl, moved to Indiana with him. At DePauw Julian both taught classes and continued his research on physostigmine.

The structure of physostigmine was known, but the chemical had never been synthesized. In 1933 Julian began publishing scientific papers describing what he believed were the precursors of physostigmine— that is, substances from which physostigmine could be formed. These were the first papers with a black person as senior author to appear in respected American chemistry journals.

Other scientists were also working on the synthesis of physostigmine. Among them was Robert Robinson, an eminent chemist at Oxford University in England. Julian suggested different precursors for physostigmine than the ones Robinson proposed. Although some people warned Julian that it was dangerous for his career to challenge such a well-established scientist as Robinson, Julian was sure he was right. He would prove it, he said, by synthesizing physostigmine from the precursors he had named.

Julian synthesized a substance that he felt sure was physostigmine. He needed to demonstrate the substance's identity, however, with one final test. If the white crystals he had synthesized were chemically the same as natural physostigmine, the two compounds would have the same melting point; that is, they would turn from solid to liquid at exactly the same temperature. One February night in 1935 Julian and Pikl prepared to test the melting point of the two compounds. Dean Blanchard was with them in the lab. At the same time, Julian, holding the test tube with the synthesized compound, and Pikl, working with natural physostigmine, began slowly raising the temperature of their materials. After a few minutes Pikl shouted, "I'm melting!" "Me too!" Julian replied. The two compounds had melted at the same moment and at the same temperature: they were identical.

Julian's successful synthesis of physostigmine guaranteed his scientific reputation. That was not the only reason that the year 1935 was important to him, however. On December 24 of that year he married Anna Johnson, a sociologist. They later had three children: Percy, Jr.; Faith; and Rhoderick.

Blanchard would have liked to appoint Julian head of DePauw's chemistry department after Julian's physostigmine triumph, but the DePauw faculty persuaded Blanchard that such a move would be "inadvisable." Julian had defied the odds by obtaining a teaching post at a white university, but clearly his chances for advancement there were limited, no matter how great his scientific reputation became.

It was thus no wonder that Julian gladly accepted when William J. O'Brien, vice-president of the Glidden Company in Chicago, phoned him in 1936 and asked him to become Glidden's director of research. Glidden was one of the country's largest producers of paints, varnishes, and related materials. By taking this job with Glidden, Julian became the first black to head a large industrial laboratory employing chemists of all races. "He was . . . a man of great energy and ability who galvanized us all," Edwin C. Meyer, one of the chemists who worked under Julian, recalled later. Meyer and most of the other Glidden chemists did not mind working under a black man as talented as Julian. "There may have been resentments that related to his color, but we were never made aware of them," Meyer noted. "We were too busy working."

Julian's work with Glidden brought him back into contact with soybeans, which he had studied briefly in Austria. Soybeans, like the peanuts that George Washington Carver worked with, are legumes. Southern farmers had always raised them to a limited extent, using them mostly to feed livestock. Although Carver had not worked with soybeans as much as with peanuts and sweet potatoes, he felt that they had great possibilities both as food for humans and as sources of industrial products. Julian now came to share this belief.

At that time casein, a protein made from milk, was used to make paints more waterproof and to coat paper so that ink put onto the paper would not smear. Casein was expensive to make, however. O'Brien asked Julian to try to find a way to make casein from soybeans. Julian did not succeed, but he did learn how to extract a soybean protein that was similar enough to casein to be used as a paper coating material. The cheap soybean substitute saved Glidden a lot of money. In Julian's first year at Glidden he oversaw the development of a new million-dollar plant for soybean protein extraction and changed the soybean division's financial picture from a $35,000 loss to a $135,000 profit.

Soybeans. Percy Julian made many useful substances from soybeans, including several hormones and a fire-smothering foam.
(Courtesy Rick Weil/Research Plus, Inc.)

Even more important soybean products followed. Julian found that certain material from the beans could be made to bubble up into a foam that "smothered" oil and gasoline fires. Fires of this kind cannot be put out with water; they must be deprived of oxygen. Julian's soybean foam was used widely to put out fires on U.S. Navy ships and crash-landed planes during World War II, and it saved countless lives. The official name of the product was Aero-Foam, but Navy men affectionately called it "bean soup." Similar fire-smothering foams are still used today.

Julian also returned to the project he had worked on in Vienna, trying to make sterols and related compounds from soybean oil. Sterols were among the members of a larger chemical family called steroids. Steroid hormones play important roles in growth, sexual development, immunity (the body's defenses against disease), and many other body functions. Supplies of these hormones would have many uses in medicine. Making the hormones from soybeans or other plants should be much cheaper than getting them from animal tissues—if it could be done.

One problem was that once the protein in soybeans was removed, the remaining oil formed a solid mass. Solvents—chemicals that might remove the sterols from the mass by turning them into a liquid form—could not penetrate the mass to reach them. Julian had no idea how to solve this problem until one day he saw an inventor friend making a compound to slow the setting of plaster. The friend added quicklime (calcium oxide) to plaster of Paris (calcium sulfate). To Julian's surprise, the resulting mixture bubbled up into a porous foam. Julian then tried adding quicklime to the solid soybean oil. Sure enough, the soybean mass also became foamy. Now Julian could add solvents and remove the sterols easily.

The first hormones that Julian produced from soybean oil, in the mid-1940s, were progesterone, a female sex hormone, and testosterone, the male sex hormone responsible for secondary sex characteristics. Progesterone was given to pregnant women who were likely to miscarry, or lose their unborn children before the babies were fully developed. The hormone allowed them to complete their pregnancies normally. Testosterone was sometimes given to older men to make them healthier and more vigorous. Today it is used to treat men with hormone imbalances and women with certain types of breast cancer.

German scientists had made progesterone and testosterone from soybeans earlier, but they had produced the hormones only in very tiny amounts. When the hormones were needed for medical treatment, they usually were made from a compound taken from the brains and spinal cords of cattle. This was a very expensive process. Julian's method of making the two hormones produced a much higher yield than these earlier processes and thus lowered the price of the hormones considerably.

Soon after cortisone's miraculous effect on arthritis was announced, Julian also learned how to make this hormone from soybeans. What he actually made was a related compound, called cortexolone or Compound S. Cortexolone contained one less oxygen atom than natural cortisone. It appeared in the adrenal glands along with cortisone, which led Julian to believe that the body could convert cortexolone to cortisone. This belief was later shown to be correct. Thus, for practical purposes, cortexolone was as good as cortisone. Julian's synthetic hormone cost only $35.00 a gram in 1951, whereas natural cortisone cost several hundred dollars a gram. Julian believed that further improvements in synthesis would bring the cost down to a few cents per gram.

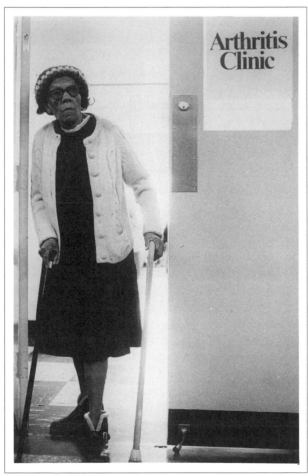

Arthritis patient. Julian's discovery of a way
to synthesize cortisone from soybeans made life less
painful and treatment less expensive for
people with arthritis.
(Courtesy The Arthritis Foundation.)

Synthetic cortisone has remained very important in medicine. It is used to treat not only arthritis but also allergies, asthma, and many other conditions in which the immune system becomes overactive. Drugstores carry inexpensive cortisone ointment that relieves the swelling, redness, and itching caused by certain insect bites or by irritating plants such as poison oak and poison ivy.

Julian left Glidden in 1953 and soon thereafter started two companies of his own, Julian Laboratories in Franklin Park (near Chicago) in 1954 and Laboratorios Julian de Mexico (in Mexico City) in 1955. Another organic chemist, Russell Marker, had learned how to extract hormone-precursor sterols from Mexican yams, and Julian formed his companies to carry out this process commercially. The yams yielded an even greater amount of sterols than soybeans had. In its first year the profit of Julian Laboratories was only $71.70, but by the second year it had grown to $97,000.

Julian sold his successful companies to a giant drug corporation, Smith, Kline, and French, in 1961 for almost $2.5 million. He started two smaller research companies, the Julian Research Institute and Julian Associates, Inc., in 1964. Julian remained in charge of these companies until his death from liver cancer on April 19, 1975.

Percy Lavon Julian published dozens of scientific papers and was awarded over a hundred patents during his working life. He also received many honors for his discoveries. The NAACP awarded him its Spingarn Medal in 1947. In 1950 he was chosen the Chicagoan of the Year in a newspaper poll. The American Institute of Chemists gave him an Honor Scroll award in 1964 and a Chemical Pioneer award in 1968. In 1990, along with George Washington Carver, Julian was elected posthumously to the National Inventors' Hall of Fame. They were the first blacks to be given this honor.

Julian was both similar to and different from Ernest Everett Just and George Washington Carver. Like Just, Julian contributed to pure scientific research. At the same time, like Carver, he used natural materials to make substances that had practical applications. Unlike Just, Julian ultimately was able to gain respected positions in both the academic and the industrial community. And unlike Carver, he was able to create products that were both commercially successful and useful to a large number of people.

The value of Percy Lavon Julian's work in terms of lives saved and health regained would be hard to overestimate. Toward the end of his life Julian said, "I have had one goal in my life, that of playing some role in making life a little easier for the persons who come after me." There can be no doubt that he succeeded.

Chronology

▬▬▬▬

April 11, 1899	Percy Lavon Julian born in Montgomery, Alabama
1916	enters DePauw University in Indiana
1920	graduates from DePauw at top of class; joins faculty of Fisk University
1923	receives master's degree in chemistry from Harvard University
1927	joins faculty of Howard University
June 1929	goes to Austria to study under chemist Ernst Spaeth
1931	receives Ph.D. degree from University of Vienna and returns to Howard
1932	leaves Howard and joins faculty of DePauw University
1933	Julian's papers on precursors of physostigmine published
February 1935	Julian synthesizes physostigmine
December 24, 1935	marries Anna Johnson
1936	becomes director of research at Glidden Company in Chicago
late 1930s	learns how to make a fire-smothering foam from soybeans
mid-1940s	synthesizes progesterone and testosterone from soybeans
1947	is awarded the NAACP's Spingarn Medal
1948	ability of cortisone to reduce pain and inflammation of arthritis discovered
c. 1949	Julian synthesizes cortexolone from soybeans
1953	leaves Glidden

1954	starts own company, Julian Laboratories
1961	sells his companies to Smith, Kline, and French
1964	starts two smaller research companies
April 19, 1975	Julian dies

Further Reading

Bims, Hamilton. "Percy L. Julian's Fight for His Life." *Ebony*, March 1975. Written near the end of Julian's life, this article provides a detailed account of his life and work.

"Carver, Julian Named to Inventors Hall of Fame." *Jet*, January 29, 1990. Short article announces this posthumous award.

De Kruif, Paul. "The Man Who Wouldn't Give Up." *Reader's Digest*, August 1946. Somewhat sentimentalized but factual account of Julian's life.

Flynn, James J. *Negroes of Achievement in Modern America*. New York: Dodd, Mead, 1970. Includes a chapter on Julian's life.

Fosdick, Franklin. "New Hope for Old Men." *Negro Digest*, March 1951. Describes Julian's synthesis of physostigmine and testosterone. Testosterone is no longer used in the manner described.

Haber, Louis. *Black Pioneers of Science and Invention*. New York: Harcourt, Brace and World, 1970. For young adults. Includes a chapter on Julian.

"Medicine's New Wonder Drugs." *Ebony*, July 1951. Mentions role of Julian and other black scientists and doctors in developing hormone treatments for arthritis and other diseases.

Wormley, Stanton L., and Fenderson, Lewis H. *Many Shades of Black*. New York: Morrow, 1969. Includes essay by Julian describing prejudice faced by past black scientists and expressing belief that this prejudice will be decreased in the future.

Charles Richard Drew
(1904–1950)

Charles Richard Drew. Drew organized the first
programs in the United States to use stored blood
and blood plasma on a large scale.
(Courtesy Moorland-Spingarn Research Center,
Howard University.)

*T*he doors of the hospital emergency room bang open, and trotting paramedics push a wheeled stretcher through them. The young woman lying on the stretcher is pale, and her skin is cold. She has been badly hurt in an auto accident and has lost a lot of blood. Her blood loss has sent her into shock: her circulatory system has collapsed because of lack of fluid. If it is not quickly reversed, shock could kill her.

The emergency room crew knows that the injured woman needs more blood as soon as possible. A nurse takes a small sample of the woman's blood and sends it to the hospital lab. From the lab a request will go to the nearest blood bank for the type of blood that the young woman needs.

Even before the blood arrives, however, the woman's shock must be treated. Another nurse therefore turns a bottle of amber fluid upside down, suspends it from a hanger, and connects it by a tube and needle to a vein in the woman's arm. The liquid in the bottle contains albumin, a chemical made from plasma, the fluid part of blood. This liquid will fill the woman's blood vessels and keep her alive until the right blood can be found.

The young woman may never know it, but indirectly she owes her life to a black surgeon, Charles Richard Drew. Drew was not the first to think of blood banks or the use of blood plasma in emergency care, but he helped to organize these lifesaving techniques on a nationwide scale. His teaching at Howard University Medical School also boosted many black surgeons into the front ranks of American surgery.

Charles Richard Drew was born on June 3, 1904, in Washington, D.C. His father, Richard, was a carpet layer. Nora, Drew's mother, spent her time caring for her five children, of whom Charlie, as everyone called him, was the oldest. The family lived in a part of the city called Foggy Bottom because of the mists from the nearby Potomac River that sometimes filled its streets. It was a racially mixed neighborhood, which was unusual: segregation was the norm in Washington, as in most other parts of the South and many parts of the North as well.

Charlie Drew was a star athlete during his high school and early college years. In Washington's highly regarded, all-black Dunbar High School he won letters in four different sports. He also won a football scholarship to Amherst, an excellent mostly white college in Massachusetts, which he entered in 1922. At Amherst Drew continued his prize-winning career in track and football. "Tuss" McLaughry, his football coach, later called Drew "the best player I ever coached."

By the time Drew graduated from Amherst, he had decided to go to medical school. However, there was no money to pay for this long and difficult training. Drew therefore took a job as coach at Morgan College, a small black college in Baltimore, Maryland. In both football and basketball, Morgan had been famous mostly for losing games, but under Drew's coaching Morgan teams began to rack up victories instead of defeats.

After two years at Morgan, Drew had saved enough money to begin medical school. However, his race barred him from all but a few medical schools in the United States. He applied first to the school at Howard University in Washington, D.C., one of the only two U.S. medical schools that concentrated on training black doctors (Meharry Medical College in Nashville was the other). Howard rejected him, saying that he had not taken enough English classes while at Amherst. Drew then applied to McGill University in Montreal, Canada, where he was accepted in 1928.

Lack of money caused problems for Drew at McGill. His father sent money when he could, but there was not much to send. Drew had to wait on tables in the school cafeteria in order to survive. "Today I haven't been hungry. . . . I am not sick and have no great sorrow, yet I have felt poverty today as I have never felt it before," he wrote on New Year's Day, 1930. "I have a dollar. Tonight I wanted to join the merry-making . . . so bad that my very heart ached. [But] I couldn't go very far on a dollar, . . . [and] I am afraid to spend it—tomorrow I must eat and the day after. . . . For days now I have not been sure whether I would eat or not."

Drew did well in his studies, however. By the time he graduated, he ranked second-highest in his class. He even continued to take prizes in football and track.One of Drew's medical school instructors was John Beattie, an Englishman several years older than he. The two men soon became friends. Beattie was very interested in the study of blood, and Drew soon came to share that interest.

The two men discussed the advances that were being made in blood research. In 1930 a scientist named Karl Landsteiner had won a Nobel Prize for work he had done in 1900 on what he called blood types. Over the centuries, doctors had occasionally tried transfusing blood from animals or healthy people into sick or injured people, but the patients had almost always died. Landsteiner had discovered why.

Landsteiner did many experiments in which he mixed red blood cells from one person with serum from another. The red cells, which carry oxygen through the body, are one of two main kinds of cells in the blood. (The oxygen is bound to a red pigment in the cells called hemoglobin.) Serum is plasma with certain chemicals removed, including those that normally make blood cells clump or clot to stop bleeding from wounds. Landsteiner found that sometimes serum caused red cells from other blood to clot and eventually destroyed them. At other times, this reaction did not occur.

Landsteiner found that the red cells of some people carried a surface chemical that he called A. The surface of some other people's cells contained a different chemical, B. The cells of a third group (called AB) contained both chemicals, and the cells of a fourth group (O) contained neither. Serum from a person with type A blood (that is, blood with red cells carrying chemical A) caused cells with the B chemical to clot. Type B serum, in turn, clotted type A cells. Serum from type O clotted both type A and type B blood, while serum from type AB did not clot any blood.

The cells of the donor and the serum of the receiver are what is important. Type O blood has been called "universal donor" blood. It can be given to people of any blood type because its cells do not contain either the A or the B chemical. This means that no receiver's serum will clot Type O cells. People with type AB blood, on the other hand, can receive transfusions from any blood type because their serum will not clot either A-containing or B-containing cells.

In short, if a person received a transfusion of blood of a type that the person's serum would not attack, the transfusion would be safe. If the transfusion was of the wrong type, however, clotted red cells from the donor blood would block blood vessels, and the person receiving the blood would probably die. Compatible and incompatible blood types appear in the chart below. (Normally a person of any blood type can safely receive a transfusion from someone else with the same blood type; these combinations are not shown.)

Transfusions Between Blood Groups

Receiver Blood	Donor Blood	Transfusion
Type A	Type B	Not OK
Type A	Type AB	Not OK
Type A	Type O	OK
Type B	Type A	Not OK
Type B	Type AB	Not OK
Type B	Type O	OK
Type AB	Type A	OK
Type AB	Type B	OK
Type AB	Type O	OK
Type O	Type A	Not OK
Type O	Type B	Not OK
Type O	Type AB	Not OK

Today scientists know that the reactions Landsteiner observed are part of the body's attempts to protect itself from invaders such as bacteria. All cell surfaces contain chemicals called antigens. The blood group chemicals that Landsteiner discovered are only a few among many possible kinds. Blood serum contains other substances known as antibodies. Different antibodies "recognize" different antigens and attach themselves to the antigens as a key fits into a lock, starting a reaction that destroys the cells on whose surfaces the antigens are located. Normally antibodies recognize and attack only antigens not found on a person's own body cells. This antigen-antibody reaction is an important part of the body's immune system.

Drew learned about blood transfusion firsthand when he gave blood for emergency transfusions at a hospital near McGill. Like other blood donors, he had to be "on call" for such emergencies, because there was no dependable way to store donated blood for later use. Sometimes he saw patients die from lack of blood because a suitable donor could not be found in time.

Charles Drew received his M.D. and master of surgery degree from McGill in 1933. He served his internship and residency, or practical training, at Montreal General Hospital. Drew's main interest, then and later, was in training other black surgeons. Therefore he applied to Howard University Medical School once again, this time asking to become a faculty member. Howard accepted him in 1935.

In 1938 Drew received a two-year Rockefeller Foundation grant for advanced training in surgery. He took this training at New York City's Columbia University and Presbyterian Hospital, where he worked under Dr. John Scudder, a well-known surgeon and researcher. It was an ideal position, for Scudder was doing research on blood transfusion, Drew's old interest from his McGill days. Scudder was trying to find a way to help surgical patients, who, like accident victims, often lost great amounts of blood and died of shock if the blood was not quickly replaced.

Safe transfusions had become possible after Landsteiner discovered blood types. People's blood type could be identified by tests, and another test, called cross-matching, was used as a final safety check before a transfusion took place. In this test, samples of a would-be donor's blood and the recipient's serum were mixed together on a glass microscope slide. If the blood did not clot, the transfusion could proceed. Cross-matching was necessary because Landsteiner and other scientists had found that red cells contained other antigens besides the A and B chemicals that Landsteiner had first identified. Sometimes serum antibodies reacted to these antigens and caused clotting even when donor's and recipient's blood were of the same or a compatible type.

Other problems remained, however. Some blood types were common, but others were more rare. As Drew had seen when he donated blood during medical school, a donor of the right type could not always be found in an emergency. A way of storing blood was desperately needed. Unfortunately, clotting chemicals in the blood's own plasma—the same chemicals that keep people from bleeding to death from any small wound—attacked the red cells soon after the blood was removed from the body and exposed to air. Once the blood began to clot, it could not be used in a transfusion. Scudder was trying to find a way to preserve blood longer, and Drew hoped to help him do so.

While at Columbia, Drew decided to study for the degree of doctor of science in medicine. No black had ever obtained this advanced degree. The topic he chose for his thesis, or long research paper, was "Banked Blood." In preparing it, he learned all he could about the attempts at blood preservation that had taken place up to that time.

There was not a lot to learn. In 1914, Drew found out, a Belgian doctor had preserved blood with a chemical called sodium citrate, which kept the blood from clotting. This chemical and similar ones were still being used. Some transfusions using stored blood had taken place during World War I. In 1937 a Chicago doctor, Bernard Fantus, had set up what he called a "blood bank," where blood could be stored for short periods. Much more extensive work with transfusions had been done in the Soviet Union, where blood from people who died in accidents and the like was routinely treated with sodium citrate and stored in refrigerated containers. However, even with this kind of treatment, whole blood could be preserved for only about 10 days. The red cells began to break down after that.

Drew and Scudder studied the chemistry of fresh blood and noted how the chemistry changed after the blood was removed from the body. To further their experiments and also to provide a source of blood for surgical patients at Presbyterian Hospital, they opened their own blood bank at the hospital in August 1939.

One volunteer medical technician at the new blood bank was a young woman named Lenore Robbins. She had joined the project specifically to be near Charles Drew. Drew had met Robbins, a home economics teacher, in Atlanta, Georgia, during the preceding April. He had asked her to marry him just three days after they met. Robbins moved to New York after a few months, and she and Drew were married on September 23, 1939.

In addition to working with whole blood, Drew and Scudder conducted experiments with blood plasma. In 1918 an English doctor had suggested using plasma rather than whole blood for emergency transfusions. More recent researchers, such as the American doctor John R. Elliott, said the same thing. Drew became more and more convinced that they were right. Plasma could not carry oxygen through the body because it lacked red cells. However, it could keep the blood vessels filled with fluid and thus prevent death from shock.

Like the researchers before him, Drew saw that plasma had many advantages over whole blood as an emergency treatment. Plasma did not contain any blood cells, so it could be given to anyone regardless of blood type. For the same reason, since the red cells were the part of blood that broke down quickly, plasma could be stored without spoiling for months rather than days. Indeed, scientists were working on ways to dry plasma to a powder so that it could be even more easily stored and shipped.

Drew used his experience with blood and plasma at the new blood bank as well as his historical research to complete his thesis on banked blood. On the basis of this thesis he received the doctor of science in medicine degree from Columbia in June 1940.

By then the study of blood transfusions was no longer just an academic exercise. War had broken out in Europe. Germany had invaded several European countries and had begun bombing cities in Great Britain. Millions of Europeans needed blood and plasma urgently.

In the same month that Drew got his degree, a New York group called the Blood Transfusion Betterment Association, with the cooperation of the American Red Cross, set up a program they called Blood for Britain. What they actually planned to send was plasma, for whole blood could not be stored long enough to be useful. Drew attended the meeting at which the program was established.

The group began shipping liquid plasma to Britain in August, but problems quickly developed. Hospitals and blood banks were not used to collecting and preserving plasma. Not all knew how to keep the liquid free of disease-causing microorganisms. Many batches of plasma were spoiled by the time they reached Britain.

It happened that the director of the British Blood Transfusion Service, which received the Blood for Britain shipments, was Drew's old friend and teacher from McGill, John Beattie. Beattie knew of Drew's continuing work on transfusion. In early September, when he learned about the spoiled shipments, Beattie sent the following telegram to the Blood Transfusion Betterment Association: "Uniform standards for all blood banks of utmost importance. Suggest you appoint overall director if program is to continue. Suggest Charles R. Drew if available."

Beattie didn't know it, but the association had already offered Drew exactly that job. Drew had returned to Howard University after obtaining his degree in June, but when he received the association's request, he asked for and was granted a four-month leave of absence. He returned to New York in late September to take over the medical directorship of the Blood for Britain program. His ability to organize others and hold them to his own high standards quickly showed itself. He set up uniform rules for collecting blood and storing plasma. He also established a central laboratory where all the plasma was sent to be examined for quality. The amount of spoiled plasma received by Britain dropped sharply.

Within a few months, after receiving 17,000 pints of American plasma, Britain was able to set up its own blood bank program and had no further need of plasma from the United States. Drew, however, found himself more in demand than ever, for many people felt sure that the United States would soon enter the war. Leaders of the U.S. armed forces asked the American Red Cross to set up a national blood bank program so that huge amounts of blood and plasma could be stockpiled for possible use by American soldiers. Drew was made medical director of the new program early in 1941.

Drew encountered many problems during the months he headed the national blood collection program, but one in particular affected him personally. At that time the United States Army did not allow black soldiers and white ones to serve together, and it extended its segregation policy even further with blood. The army refused to accept any blood from black donors. (Later, after the United States had joined the war, the army accepted blacks' blood but kept the blood segregated, giving it only to black soldiers.)

Drew's wife later remembered that he called a press conference to express his disgust at this policy. "The blood of individual human beings may differ by groupings [types], but there is absolutely no

Charles Drew (left) with staff of the first mobile blood unit.
The "Bloodmobile" was Drew's invention.
(Courtesy Moorland-Spingarn Research Center, Howard University.)

scientific basis to indicate any difference according to race," he told reporters. There was thus no medical reason why someone of one race could not safely receive blood or plasma from someone of another race.

Drew resigned from the directorship of the blood bank program and returned to Howard University in early April 1941. He felt that the blood program could now go on without him, and he was anxious to get back to what he always considered his most important work: training young black surgeons. He said in later years that his blood work fame, along with his success as a college football star, was something he wished he could "live down."

Drew was quickly made professor of surgery at Howard and chief surgeon at the medical school's affiliated hospital, Freedmen's Hospital. In 1944 he became the hospital's chief of staff. He and his wife got their own house and, for the first time, settled down. Over the years they had four children: Bebe (for "BB," short for "blood bank"—born about the time that the Blood for Britain program started), Charlene, Rhea Sylvia, and Charles, Jr.

Drew now concentrated on making the surgeons who trained under him good enough to compete against any others in the country. Unlike Ernest Just and Percy Julian, he enjoyed teaching at Howard. Like Daniel Williams, Drew held his surgical students to high standards. "That man was a perfectionist from the first day I met him," recalled Dr. Samuel Bullock, a fellow surgeon at Freedmen's who had known Drew since high school. "He thrived on doing things—and having others do them—that he could take pride in."

"Dream high," Lenore Drew remembered her husband urging his classes at Howard. "We're going to turn out surgeons here who will not have to apologize to *anybody, anywhere!*"

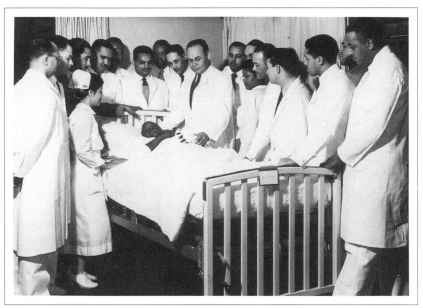

Drew teaching a class at Freedmen's Hospital. Training top-quality black surgeons was Drew's chief interest.
(Courtesy Moorland-Spingarn Research Center, Howard University.)

Charles Drew received many awards for his scientific work, including the NAACP's Spingarn Medal (in 1944) and the E. S. Jones Award for Research in Medical Science. Even more important to him, however, was the success of his students. More than half of the black surgeons receiving certification from the American Board of Surgery between 1941 and 1950 studied under Drew. Many of his students did pioneering work in new surgical subspecialties such as urology (treatment of the excretory system). Several became chiefs of surgery or medical directors of hospitals in various parts of the country.

Unfortunately, Drew's years as a scientist and teacher were cut short. On April 1, 1950, when Drew was only 45 years old, he set out by car with several other doctors for a medical conference in Tuskegee, Alabama. Drew drove, although he had had only two hours' sleep the night before. Sometime in the early morning the car went off the road. The other doctors were not severely injured, but Drew was crushed. He died soon after reaching the nearest hospital.

Charles Drew may have been right in believing that his teaching work at Howard was at least as important as his better-known work with blood preservation. He was, in a way, the Daniel Hale Williams of his day. One of his students, Dr. Charles D. Watts, later said, "He helped prepare a whole generation of surgeons, and a whole new thrust in training."

Nonetheless, it was not surprising that Charles Drew never "lived down" his work with blood banks and blood plasma. Dr. John Scudder, under whom Drew had done his blood research, called him not only "my most brilliant student, but one of the greatest clinical scientists of the first half of the twentieth century." Clyde E. Buckingham of the American Red Cross wrote that in organizing the wartime blood bank program, Drew showed "exceptional ability in synthesizing the work of others . . . , organizing such data into a workable process, which made possible a major step forward toward the goal of mass production of blood supplies in the large quantities and in the form which could be used by the armed forces under conditions of modern warfare."

Although Drew did not originate the idea of storing blood or of using plasma for emergencies, he applied these ideas on a large scale for the first time in the United States. Like Percy Julian and George Washington Carver, he turned pure science into a form that could help large numbers of people. The national program that Drew headed became the model for the American Red Cross's volunteer blood donation program and for blood banks throughout the country. Drew's work shaped blood bank standards and policy for many years to come and was responsible for saving millions of lives.

Chronology

June 3, 1904	Charles Richard Drew born in Washington, D.C.
1922	enters Amherst College
1926	graduates from Amherst and becomes coach at Morgan College
1928	enters medical school at McGill University in Montreal, Canada
1933	gains M.D. and master of surgery degrees from McGill
1935	joins faculty of Howard University Medical School
1938	gets grant to take advanced training in surgery at Columbia University and Presbyterian Hospital in New York City
1939	Drew and Scudder open their own blood bank
Sept. 23, 1939	Drew marries Lenore Robbins
June 1940	receives doctor of science in medicine degree from Columbia; Blood for Britain program begins
September 1940	takes over medical directorship of Blood for Britain program
January 1941	is made medical director of Red Cross national blood collection program
April 1941	resigns from Red Cross program and returns to Howard
1944	is made chief of staff at Freedmen's Hospital; receives Spingarn Medal from NAACP
April 1, 1950	Drew killed in automobile accident

Further Reading

Quotations from the Charles R. Drew Papers are reprinted by permission of the Manuscript Division of the Moorland-Spingarn Research Center, Howard University.

Bims, Hamilton. "Charles Drew's 'Other' Medical Revolution." *Ebony*, February 1974. Describes Drew's life with an emphasis on his teaching and the later success of his students.

Drew, Lenore Robbins. "Unforgettable Charlie Drew." *Reader's Digest*, March 1978. Memoir of Drew by his wife.

Haber, Louis. *Black Pioneers of Science and Invention*. New York: Harcourt, Brace & World, Inc., 1970. For young adults. Devotes a chapter to Drew.

Hardwick, Richard. *Charles Richard Drew: Pioneer in Blood Research*. New York: Charles Scribner's Sons, 1967. For young adults. Contains fictionalized material and overstates Drew's achievements to some extent.

McLaughry, D. O. (Tuss). "The Best Player I Ever Coached." *Saturday Evening Post*, December 6, 1952. In this brief article, Drew's coach at Amherst shows that Drew as a football player had characteristics that were important in his later life.

Mahone-Lonesome, Robyn. *Charles R. Drew: Physician*. New York: Chelsea House, 1990. A full-length biography of Drew written for young adults.

Page, Jake. *Blood: The River of Life*. Washington, D.C.: U.S. News Books, 1981. Provides background on blood and blood transfusions.

Wynes, Charles E. *Charles Richard Drew: The Man and the Myth*. Urbana and Chicago: The University of Illinois Press, 1988. Probably the only adult, nonfictionalized biography of Drew; dispels "myths" about him that appear in other books.

Jane Cooke Wright
(1919–)

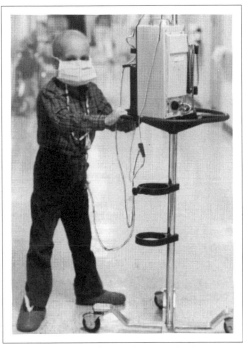

*Boy receiving chemotherapy. Anticancer
drugs have made this boy's hair
fall out temporarily, but they are likely
to save his life.*
(Courtesy Leukemia Society of America.)

A few months ago the boy in the hospital seemed just like any
other five-year-old, playing tag and catch with his friends. Then,
however, he became weak and sick. He felt tired all the time, and
he seemed to catch every cold or other "bug" that his playmates
had. Any time he fell or bumped himself, he developed a big
bruise.

The boy's parents took him to the family doctor, who drew a sample of the boy's blood and sent it to a laboratory for analysis. When the lab results came back, the doctor called the boy's parents back to her office. Her face was grave. The boy, she said, had leukemia, a kind of blood cancer. The white cells in his blood, instead of maturing and doing their normal job of fighting disease, remained immature and were multiplying wildly.

If this scene in the doctor's office had taken place 30 years ago, the doctor would have gone on to say that the boy probably had only a few months to live. Today, however, the story's ending is likely to be different.

To be sure, the boy and his parents have a hard few months ahead of them. He has to go to the hospital to receive chemotherapy, or drug treatment, for his cancer. A combination of powerful anticancer medications are dripped into his bloodstream through a tube. For a while, the drugs may seem to make him sicker than the leukemia. He may feel sick to his stomach and vomit. His hair may fall out. He will have to wear a mask to protect him from disease-causing microorganisms in the air because the drugs will weaken his immune system.

At the end of the course of chemotherapy treatments, though, the chances are very high—90 percent—that the boy's leukemia will be stopped, or put into remission. The remission may last for years. The boy's hair will grow back, and his strength will return. Indeed, he has a 50 percent chance of having his cancer cured completely and going on to lead a normal life.

This boy and the millions of other cancer patients whose lives have been saved or prolonged by chemotherapy owe much to the work of a black doctor and scientist named Jane Cooke Wright. Wright helped to test a wide variety of anticancer drugs on people with different kinds of cancer that formerly could not be treated. She also worked out a way to screen chemicals for anticancer activity and to find out which drugs were most likely to be successful in a particular patient.

———

Jane Cooke Wright was born on November 30, 1919, in New York City. Her father, Louis Tompkins Wright, was a famous black surgeon who was interested in cancer. At the time Jane Wright was born, Louis Wright was working as a surgeon at Harlem Hospital. Harlem in those days was a wealthy white community, and Louis Wright was the first black doctor to be appointed to Harlem Hospital's staff (or, indeed, the staff of any New York City hospital). In time he became the hospital's director of surgery and, later, president of its medical board.

Louis Wright was the first black doctor to head a public interracial hospital (Provident, the hospital that Daniel Hale Williams founded, was private), the first black surgeon to work in the New York City police department, and the first black surgeon to be admitted to the American College of Surgeons since Daniel Hale Williams had helped to found it. Like Charles Drew, though much more briefly, he also worked at Freedmen's Hospital in Washington, D.C.

Given Jane Wright's family background, it was no surprise that she became a doctor. After going to elementary and high school in New York City, she went to college at Smith, a highly respected college in Massachusetts. At first, like George Washington Carver, she was more interested in painting than medicine. She was also a star swimmer, setting records that went unbroken for many years. Her father discouraged her from considering a career in painting, however, pointing out that art was a risky way to earn a living. (The same thing had occurred to Carver.) After changing to a premedical major, Wright graduated from Smith in 1942.

Jane Wright insisted in later years that her father never pressured her to study medicine; indeed, he warned her how hard becoming a doctor would be. His very fame made her training harder in some ways. "His being so good really makes it very difficult," Wright told an interviewer soon after she graduated from medical school. "You feel you have to do better. Everyone knows who Papa is." His example must have had strong positive effects as well, however, because not only Jane but her younger sister, Barbara, chose to earn medical degrees. Jane Wright received her M.D. degree with honors from New York Medical College in 1945, having been chosen vice-president of her class and president of the honor society. Her sister graduated a year later from the Physicians and Surgeons College of Columbia University and went into industrial medicine.

Jane Wright took her practical medical training (internship and residency) at New York's large Bellevue Hospital and, later, at Harlem Hospital. Her supervisor at Bellevue later said that she was the most promising intern who had ever worked with him. In 1947 Wright married David D. Jones, a lawyer who became prominent in antipoverty and job training groups for young black people in New York City. Wright took six months off from her residency training to have her first child, Jane. She and Jones later had another daughter, Alison. Jones died of a heart attack in 1976.

Jane Cooke Wright and Barbara Wright (left to right) soon after completing medical school. Her father's example inspired Jane Wright to develop better drug treatments for cancer.
(Courtesy Moorland-Spingarn Research Center, Howard University, and "Headlines and Pictures.")

In 1948 Wright's father established the Cancer Research Foundation at Harlem Hospital. There he became a pioneer in the development of cancer chemotherapy. Jane Wright originally planned a career in general internal medicine, but after her father invited her to join him at the foundation in 1949, she came to share his interest in chemotherapy. For several years father and daughter did research on cancer drugs together.

At that time, chemotherapy had existed as a medical field for only a few years. Throughout history, to be sure, doctors from time to time had tried treating cancerous growths or tumors with chemicals, using such substances as arsenic paste, corrosive acids, and ground-up toads. These treatments occasionally succeeded in "burning off" small tumors, but for the most part they were as unsuccessful as they must have been painful. Early in the 20th century, doctors had discovered that a few cancers depended on hormones and could be controlled or cured if the source of hormones was removed. Some women with breast cancer, for example, were treated by removing their ovaries, the main source of female hormones. In other cancer cases, giving hormones caused some improvement. Successful treatment of cancer with chemicals that did not come from the body, however, began only in the 1940s.

The first chemical destined to save the lives of cancer patients was originally invented to destroy lives in war. Called nitrogen mustard, it was a relative of mustard gas, one of several chemical weapons used in World War I. Mustard gas blistered the skin of soldiers exposed to it.

Although European countries had vowed after World War I never again to use chemical weapons like mustard gas, some of the gas was prepared for possible use during World War II. In 1942 a U.S. ship carrying mustard gas was sunk accidentally in the harbor of Bari, Italy. The escaping gas fatally poisoned many sailors on the ship. Doctors noticed that, among other things, the gas seemed to destroy most of the white cells in the sailors' blood. These were the same cells that multiplied uncontrollably in leukemia. Someone wondered if some less toxic chemical relative of the gas might be used to treat leukemia and other blood cell cancers. Many related chemicals were tested in animals, and in 1946 two doctors reported the first successful treatment of a human cancer patient with nitrogen mustard. The compound was injected into a vein as a liquid.

Nitrogen mustard and drugs related to it form one family of anticancer drugs, the alkylating agents. They change the chemical nature of certain important molecules in cells. Like radiation, which is also used to treat cancer, this group of drugs damages cancer cells' reproductive mechanisms and usually goes on to kill the cells.

Partly because cancer cells grow rapidly, they are more suscep-
tible to damage by alkylating agents than normal cells are. The
drugs are toxic to normal cells, too, however. This is true of most
anticancer drugs. Because the dose of an anticancer drug that kills
a tumor and the dose that causes unwanted, harmful side effects
by damaging normal cells are usually very similar, the amounts
given to patients must be calculated very carefully. (Fast-growing
normal cells, such as those in hair shafts and the lining of the
digestive system, are the most likely to be harmed by anticancer
drugs. This is why people receiving chemotherapy often have
upset stomachs and lose their hair.) Cancer cells differ so little
from normal cells that finding a drug that will kill one but not the
other is almost impossible.

Louis and Jane Wright tested new alkylating agents, such as
triethylenemelamine (TEM), on cancer patients. They continued
to work together until Louis Wright's death in 1952. Jane Wright
then took over her father's position as head of the Cancer Research
Foundation. In 1955 she joined the faculty of New York University, where she eventually became associate professor of research
surgery. She continued her cancer research as well, acting as
director of chemotherapy at the university's medical center.

Wright took a break from her cancer research work in 1961 to
visit the East African countries of Kenya and Tanganyika (now
Tanzania) as part of a medical team sponsored by the African
Research Foundation. She and four other doctors, along with a
nurse and other assistants, spent three weeks traveling through
the African countryside in a mobile medical unit, a sort of hospital
on wheels. This vehicle contained medical supplies and equipment, including an x-ray machine, and had its own electricity and
running water. It acted as a combined examining room, laboratory, school, and operating room.

Wright and the other doctors treated 341 people during their
week in Kenya alone, visiting many areas where modern medical
care was unknown. In addition to providing medical treatment,
the group gave out food supplements and instructed people in
ways to improve their health. Although Wright herself could not
devote any more time to this project, she believed strongly that
more mobile medical units like the one she had joined should
travel through Africa. She continued to support the African Research Foundation and later became its vice president.

In the 1950s and 1960s Wright treated cancer patients with a
variety of drugs, always seeking the particular type or types of

chemotherapy that would most successfully battle each patient's disease. She tested several different "families" of anticancer drugs, each of which attacked cancer cells in a different way. Alkylating agents such as nitrogen mustard make up one chemotherapeutic family. Another family is the antimetabolites, which mimic nutrients that the cancer cells must have in order to survive. The cells take up these "fakes" instead of the compounds they need and thus, in effect, starve to death. Antitumor antibiotics make up a third family. Like streptomycin and many other antibiotics that are used to treat bacterial infections, these substances come from microorganisms that live in the soil. Instead of attacking bacteria, however, they attack cancer cells. Anticancer compounds in other drug "families" come from plants, metal salts, and even undersea creatures such as sponges.

One drug that Wright tested was mithramycin, an anticancer antibiotic produced by a soil mold related to the mold that makes streptomycin. She used mithramycin to treat people with a kind of brain tumor called glioblastoma. This type of tumor normally kills patients within a few months, even if they have been treated with surgery and radiation. Brain tumors of any kind are very difficult to treat with drugs because most substances that circulate in the bloodstream, including drugs, are kept from entering the brain by a sort of natural filter called the blood-brain barrier. Mithramycin, however, was able to cross this barrier and reach the tumors.

In a 1965 report, Wright and other doctors described treating 14 glioblastoma patients with mithramycin. None of the patients had severe side effects, and eight showed some improvement and extension of life. Of these eight, three showed major improvement. A 26-year-old woman, for example, had been made dizzy, confused, and partly paralyzed on one side by her tumor. After two courses of mithramycin treatment, however, she was alert and cheerful. She could walk by herself and do most everyday tasks. She was still alive and had no signs of cancer at the time the report was written, almost two years after her treatment.

In July 1967, Wright returned to her old school, New York Medical College. "Coming back gave me a marvelous feeling," she said. She became professor of surgery and associate dean, the highest post in medical administration obtained by a black woman. She also directed the college's newly established cancer research laboratory. She remained in these jobs until she retired in 1987. She also continued her clinical work at Lincoln Hospital and several other New York City hospitals and medical centers.

As more and more compounds with anticancer activity were discovered, deciding which drug to use on a particular patient became an increasingly important challenge. Different kinds of cancers responded to different drugs, and even the same kind of cancer responded differently in different people. The wrong choice of drug could waste precious time on an ineffective treatment, cause a patient unnecessary suffering, or both. Therefore, between 1953 and 1975, Wright worked out ways to use pieces of a patient's own tumor, removed by surgery and grown in nutrient culture medium in the laboratory, as a "guinea pig" for testing drugs. Groups of cells grown in this way are called tissue cultures.

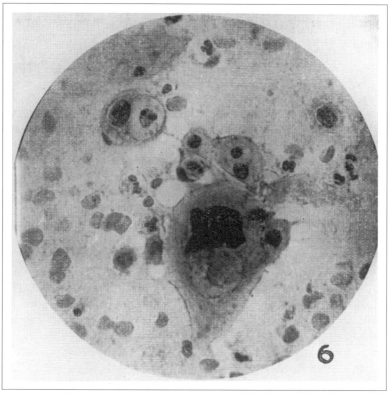

Cancer cells. Jane Wright found that examining cancer cells grown in tissue culture could help to predict which drugs would be most effective against that cancer. These cells are from the cervix, or neck of the uterus.
(Courtesy American Cancer Society.)

After cultures of tumor cells were treated with the drugs, they were examined under a microscope for signs of damage. Wright found that drugs that killed the cells of a particular tumor in culture usually killed that tumor in the patient as well. Similarly, drugs that were ineffective in culture also were ineffective when given to the patient.

The tissue culture method is useful in another way, Wright has pointed out. New compounds suspected of having anticancer activity have usually been tested on animals with tumors. Testing with animals, however, is slow and expensive. Furthermore, because of differences between human beings and laboratory test animals such as mice (for instance, mice can tolerate doses of some anticancer drugs 20 times higher in proportion to body weight than the doses that people can stand), some drugs that work in the animals don't work in people. Testing the drugs on human tumor cells in tissue culture is much cheaper and more efficent than using animals, Wright has noted, and the results are more likely to reflect what will happen when people are given the drugs in a hospital. Studying the cells in culture also shows precisely how the different drugs attack the tumors. Some of the methods Wright worked out for testing drugs on cells in tissue culture are still used. They allow treatment to be tailored precisely to each patient.

Based on her work with a wide variety of anticancer compounds over the years, Wright developed a "philosophy" or general approach to treating cancer patients with these drugs. She began treatment with a low dose of drug, then slowly increased the dose either until the tumor began to shrink or until the patient began to experience significant side effects such as kidney or liver damage. If toxic side effects appeared, treatment was stopped at once. It was started up again at a lower dose once the side effects decreased. If a tumor was going to respond to treatment with a particular drug, Wright found that it would usually begin to shrink after between six and eight weeks of treatment. However, the greatest possible effect of the drug might not show until treatment had been continued for six months or a year.

If side effects did not occur and the cancer responded to the treatment, Wright continued to give the drug at as high a dose as the patient could stand for as long as cancer cells continued to be found in the person's body. Some patients were treated for as long as nine years. During that time the dosage of drug was likely to have to be adjusted many times, because drug tolerance varied not only from person to person but in the same person at different times. Deciding how often to give doses of the drugs also required careful consideration.

Wright served on a number of advisory boards and joined many professional societies during her career. In the early 1960s she was a member of the President's Commission on Heart Disease, Cancer, and Stroke. She worked on the editorial board of the *Journal of the National Medical Association* and was secretary-treasurer of the American Society of Clinical Oncology (oncology is the study and treatment of cancer). She also was a member of the Manhattan Council of the State Commission on Human Rights.

Wright received many awards for her work in cancer chemotherapy. The Albert Einstein School of Medicine gave her the Spirit of Achievement Award, for example. Several universities awarded her honorary doctorates, and the National Council of Negro Women gave her a distinguished service award. In 1975 the American Association for Cancer Research officially saluted her for important contributions to research in cancer chemotherapy, an award she has said that she values above all others.

Work with anticancer drugs has always been an exciting challenge for Jane Wright. She values the feeling of discovery and adventure that it gives her, as well as the knowledge that she is working on an important problem. She is depressed when patients die in spite of treatment but thrilled when the drugs make tumors vanish.

Wright calls chemotherapy the "Cinderella" of cancer research because it is a relatively recent form of treatment and, at least at first, was not widely used by doctors. However, she points out that chemotherapy has been in use for several decades and now is considered quite respectable. More than 50 anticancer drugs are now in regular use. Like the hormones that Percy Julian synthesized and the national blood banks that Charles Drew helped to establish, the anticancer drugs that Jane Wright helped to test have saved or prolonged the lives of millions.

The new thrust in chemotherapy, Wright explains, is to use combinations of drugs. This approach, called polychemotherapy (*poly-* means "many"), has replaced the earlier idea that a single "magic bullet" drug would be found that could cure all cancers or even all cancers of a particular type. Combination drug therapy allows tumor cells to be attacked by several means at once (both blocking their reproduction and depriving them of nutrients, for example). It also means that individual drugs can be given at lower doses, thus minimizing side effects, and that a tumor is less likely to become drug resistant, which is a common problem in cancer treatment. Treatment with combinations of drugs often is given after initial treatment with surgery or radiation to "mop up" cancer cells left behind by the other treatments and minimize the chance of a tumor's spread or recurrence. Regular schedules of polychemotherapy, called by acronymic titles (formed from the first letters of the names of the drugs used) such as MOPP, POMP, VAMP, and BIKE, have been worked out for a number of common cancers. The possible drug combinations, Wright says, are "almost unlimited."

Wright has not felt that being either black or a woman has held back her career. She is also proud that she was able to combine full-time medical research with raising a family. As she once told an audience of young women, she could not imagine a better way of life.

Chronology

November 30, 1919	Jane Cooke Wright born in New York City
1942	graduates from Smith College
1945	receives M.D. degree with honors from New York Medical College
1947	marries David D. Jones
1949	joins her father at Cancer Research Foundation
1952	takes over directorship of Cancer Research Foundation after her father's death
1955	joins faculty of New York University
1961	visits East Africa as part of a medical team sponsored by the African Research Foundation
1965	reports tests of mithramycin in patients with brain tumors
July 1967	becomes professor of surgery and associate dean of New York Medical College
1960s, 1970s	develops tissue culture tests for anticancer drugs
1975	American Association for Cancer Research salutes Wright's research in cancer in chemotherapy
1987	Wright retires from post at New York Medical College

Further Reading

Afro-American Encyclopedia, Vol. 10. N. Miami, Fla.:Educational Book Publishers, Inc., 1974. Provides a brief factual sketch of Jane Wright's life and work.

"Beauty Goes Medical." *Headlines and Pictures*, May 1946. Includes interviews with Jane Wright and her sister, Barbara, just after they finished medical school.

Cloyd, Iris, ed. *Who's Who Among Black Americans* (6th ed., 1990–91). Detroit: Gale Research, Inc., 1990. Brief listing gives basic facts about Wright's life.

Haber, Louis. *Women Pioneers of Science*. New York: Harcourt Brace Jovanovich, 1979. For young adults. Chapter gives details of Wright's life and includes an interview with her.

Hayden, Robert C., and Jacqueline Harris. *Nine Black American Doctors*. Reading, Mass.: Addison-Wesley, 1976. For young adults. Chapter on Wright has less detail than that in Haber book and covers somewhat different material.

Ransohoff, Joseph, and others. "Preliminary Clinical Study of Mithramycin (NSC-24559) in Primary Tumors of the Central Nervous System." *Cancer Chemotherapy Reports*, December 1965. Describes test of mithramycin as treatment for brain tumors.

Wright, Jane C. "Cancer Chemotherapy: Past, Present, and Future, Part I." *Journal of the National Medical Association*, August 1984. First part of Wright's review of cancer chemotherapy includes improvements in cancer survival, history of chemotherapy, and description of several anticancer drug "families."

Wright, Jane C. "Cancer Chemotherapy: Past, Present, and Future, Part II." *Journal of the National Medical Association*, September 1984. Second part of Wright's review of cancer chemotherapy includes description of polychemotherapy, tissue culture tests to determine anticancer drug effectiveness, and Wright's general approach to using chemotherapy.

Bertram O. Fraser-Reid
(1934–   )

*Bertram Fraser-Reid with a model of a
molecule of amphotericin. This antibiotic,
used to treat yeast infections, is just one
of the many complex molecules that
Fraser-Reid has analyzed.*
(Courtesy Bertram O. Fraser-Reid.)

A man finds out that he has been infected with the AIDS virus.
Before he can become sick, however, a doctor gives him a drug
that keeps a certain chemical on the outside of the virus from
breaking down. The virus cannot infect cells unless this chemical
breaks down. As long as the man keeps taking the drug, the virus
in his body will remain powerless.

Pest insects attack the trees of a northern forest. Instead of spraying the forest with deadly insecticides, government scientists set off a "bomb" that releases a chemical slowly into the air over a period of weeks. The chemical is an artificial form of one made by the insects' own bodies. It does not harm plants, birds, or animals. It lures the pest insects into traps where they are killed.

The economy of a small Central American country is hurt because the country needs to import petroleum at a high cost. It needs the petroleum not only for fuel but for manufacturing a variety of compounds, including plastics and medicines. Its economic picture is improved when advisers show the leaders of its industries how to make these compounds from sugarcane, which grows so easily in the country that it is almost a waste product, instead of from petroleum.

These scenarios are not actual, but they, or similar ones, may occur in the future. If they do, their successful outcome is likely to be traceable partly to the work of black scientist Bertram O. Fraser-Reid. Like Percy Julian, Fraser-Reid is an organic chemist. His special field is the study of the family of organic compounds called sugars or carbohydrates. He has discovered new ways to synthesize carbohydrates. He also has found ways to use carbohydrates to make chemicals that are not carbohydrates.

The carbohydrate that most people know best is the sugar that they sprinkle on their cereal or stir into their tea. In fact, however, many other foods, from fruits and vegetables to bread and pasta, contain carbohydrates. Carbohydrates are the chief source of energy in the diets of most animals, including humans. They also play an important part in helping body cells function and communicate with each other. Because carbohydrates are so important to living things, Fraser-Reid's work has many possible applications. It may help scientists learn about the causes and perhaps cures of diseases such as AIDS, diabetes, and cancer. It also may be important in industry and agriculture.

———

Bertram Fraser-Reid was born on the Caribbean island of Jamaica on February 23, 1934. He had five older brothers and sisters. William, his father, was an elementary school principal. Bert's mother, Laura, was a teacher. She died when Bert was only nine months old.

Black Scientists

At first, Bert Fraser-Reid followed his parents' footsteps into teaching. Because the school system in Jamaica is arranged a little differently from that of the United States, he had had the equivalent of about a year of college by the time he finished high school at age 17. He became "junior master" in a secondary school, teaching a variety of subjects. He taught in Jamaica for five years. He thought he might go on to a career in music. Playing the pipe organ and piano is still one of his favorite activities.

Bert Fraser-Reid's plans for a musical career changed, however, after he met Stanley Shepherd, a young Jamaican who had studied in Britain and returned to the island to teach science in the school where Fraser-Reid taught. The two men became friends. Shepherd enjoyed teaching physics and mathematics but hated chemistry. In discussing it, however, Fraser-Reid found that he felt very differently, even though he had never studied chemistry before. "I was fascinated with what he was doing—the practical side of things," he recalls. "Chemistry is what you do with your hands. Chemists make things. That's exciting." Fraser-Reid's interest was so great that he bought a book called *Teach Yourself Chemistry* and proceeded to do precisely that.

Fraser-Reid decided that he wanted to study chemistry more systematically in college. Partly because he was concerned about violence against blacks in the United States, he chose to go to Canada. He enrolled in Queen's University in Kingston, Ontario in 1956. He got his bachelor of science degree three years later.

While Fraser-Reid was still an undergraduate he decided that he wanted to get some experience in chemical research. At that time J. K. N. Jones, a famous chemist who specialized in the study of carbohydrates, worked at Queen's. Fraser-Reid arranged to become an assistant in Jones's lab, and he soon picked up Jones's "infectious" enthusiasm for the large and complex carbohydrate family.

The word *carbohydrate* means "watered carbon." Carbohydrates are combinations of carbon, hydrogen, and oxygen. The chemical name for the simplest group of carbohydrates or sugars (those that cannot be broken down into simpler ones) is *monosaccharides*. Glucose, the sugar that makes corn syrup, honey, and certain other foods taste sweet, is a monosaccharide. So is fructose, the sugar that makes many fruits sweet. Glucose and fructose, in fact, have the same chemical formula ($C_6H_{12}O_6$), but their molecules are arranged differently. Sucrose, or white table sugar, is a disaccharide, a combination of one glucose and one fructose molecule. Carbohydrates containing three to six monosaccharides are called oligosaccharides, and those containing more than six are called polysaccharides. Carbohydrates are probably the most widespread organic substances in nature. They are vital to all living things.

Fraser-Reid continued to study with Jones until he got his master's degree. Then, in 1961, he went to the University of Alberta, in Edmonton, to study for his Ph.D. There he joined a laboratory very different from Jones's, headed by Raymond U. Lemieux. Lemieux was analyzing complex carbohydrates by a technique called nuclear magnetic resonance (NMR) that was very new at that time. Today this technique, sometimes called magnetic resonance imaging (MRI), is used in medicine as well as in chemistry and other fields. Lemieux was the first person to use NMR in carbohydrate chemistry, and Fraser-Reid helped him develop this new tool.

NMR works because the nuclei in some atoms act like little spinning magnets. When placed in a strong magnetic field, the nuclei in these atoms line up, just as iron filings line up when placed near a magnet. They do not line up entirely straight, however. The axis of each nucleus (an imaginary line that runs through the center of the nucleus) wobbles or precesses a little in a random direction.

Once the nuclei have lined up, an oscillating or vibrating magnetic field is introduced at right angles to the first field. This makes all the atoms wobble together in the same direction. When this second field is turned off, the nuclei slowly return to their random wobble. As they do so they send out electric signals that can be detected and stored in a computer.

The nuclei of different kinds of atoms, or the same atoms in different chemical arrangements (a hydrogen atom in a water molecule and a hydrogen atom in a hydrogen peroxide molecule, for example), change back to a random wobble at different rates and therefore send out different signals. The computer can analyze the signals to give chemical information about the material being tested. NMR works in medicine because the chemicals in, for example, cancer cells are a little different from those in normal cells.

Lemieux and Fraser-Reid used NMR to analyze the structure of complex carbohydrates more precisely than had ever been possible before. This was important because, in order to synthesize these complicated compounds, scientists have to know not only what atoms they contain but how those atoms are arranged. As with sucrose and fructose, different arrangements of the same atoms can produce compounds with different characteristics.

While working with Lemieux in Edmonton, Fraser-Reid ran into Lillian Lawrynyuk, a young Ukrainian-Canadian woman he had known while he was at Queen's University. She was working as a nurse in a government hospital for Indians and Eskimos in Edmonton. Although the two had not dated at Queen's, they became more than friends now. They were married in 1963. They later had two children, Andrea and Terry.

After obtaining his Ph.D. in 1964, Fraser-Reid went to London, England, to work in the laboratory of Sir Derek Barton at Imperial College. Barton later won a Nobel Prize in chemistry. "I'd worked in carbohydrates for my Master's and my Ph.D., and I wanted to learn something totally different," Fraser-Reid recalls. With Barton he studied the chemistry of the way oxygen is added to compounds.

Fraser-Reid did not make any important discoveries in Barton's lab, but he remembers his years there as one of the most exciting times of his life. "The main advantage of being in Barton's lab was the training," he says. "There were so many talented people around, and it was a very stimulating environment. Chemists are made because of who they talk to. That's where you learn chemistry. Being challenged and rising to new heights—that's what chemistry's all about."

In 1966 Fraser-Reid returned to Canada and joined the faculty of the University of Waterloo, a new university just outside of Toronto. It was there that he had one of his most important ideas. He was still interested in carbohydrates, but his work in Barton's lab had led him to look at these compounds in a new way. He knew that carbohydrates were only one of the "families" of compounds in organic chemistry. Others included steroids (the family Percy Julian had worked with), alkaloids, and terpenes. "Normally, if you're interested in one of these families, you work within that family," Fraser-Reid explains. "But my exposure in Barton's lab had led me to the idea that one could cross these boundaries. I realized that sugars were good not only for making other sugars but for making a whole host of other things as well." Fraser-Reid had this realization, he says, when he was talking to one of his then graduate students, David Hicks. "Students or research workers have always been very instrumental in changing the way I do things," he points out.

Bertram O. Fraser-Reid

In 1975 Fraser-Reid became the first to publish a method for using simple sugars to make nonsugar compounds. Two years later he won the Merck, Sharpe & Dohme award for making outstanding contributions to organic chemistry in Canada largely because of this research.

Fraser-Reid's idea was important for several reasons. For one thing, it meant that any compound that could be made from petroleum could theoretically be made from sugars instead. A huge number of valuable chemicals are made from petroleum, including plastics, medicines, and substances used in industry. Although Fraser-Reid plays down the industrial possibilities of his idea, others have suggested that it could be useful to countries, such as some in Central and South America, that easily grow sugarcane but have to import all their petroleum. In a world where petroleum supplies are vanishing quickly, it eventually may be useful to everyone.

Fraser-Reid points out another use of his process that may be even more important: making chemicals pure to a degree that was never possible before. The complex molecules of many organic chemicals, he explains, "are like a pair of gloves. One is right-handed, the other is left-handed." Put another way, the molecules are mirror images of each other. Although the mirror-image molecules are considered to be the same chemical, they can have properties that differ in significant ways.

Often, one form of such a molecule is chemically active (effective as a drug, say) while the mirror-image form is inactive. Sometimes, however, the molecules are active in dramatically different ways. For example, Fraser-Reid remembers a sleeping drug called thalidomide that caused severe birth defects when taken by pregnant women. The drug was taken off the market in the early 1960s. The birth defects happened, Fraser-Reid says, because some of the molecules in the thalidomide were the wrong "glove."

Making chemicals that contain molecules of only one of the two possible mirror-image forms is important in many processes. When chemicals are synthesized from petroleum, Fraser-Reid explains, both forms of molecule usually are produced. They must then be separated. When the chemicals are made from sugars, however, only one form or the other is produced. Thus, potentially at least, making chemicals from sugars is a simpler process and results in purer material.

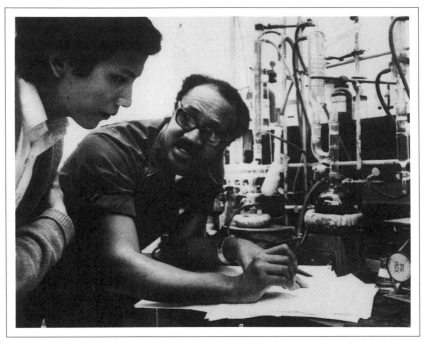

Bertram O. Fraser-Reid with a graduate student. Making pure substances is very important in organic chemistry. The machines in this picture help chemists make pure solvents.
(Courtesy Bertram O. Fraser-Reid.)

One of the most interesting molecules that Fraser-Reid synthesized with his new process showed the promise of becoming an important weapon in the war against destructive insect pests, particularly those that attacked trees. One day in 1975 a scientist named Ian Weatherstone, who worked for the Canadian Forestry Service, came to the University of Waterloo to give a talk on problems caused by the insecticide DDT. DDT, once hailed as a "miracle" destroyer of insect pests, had just been banned in Canada because scientists had discovered that it greatly harmed the environment. (It also has been banned in the United States.)

Scientists were looking for ways to destroy pest insects without using insecticides. One approach to the problem involved pheromones, complex chemicals made in the insects' bodies that send messages to other insects when the chemicals are released into the environment. (Animals besides insects also release pheromones.) One kind of pheromone is broadcast into the air by insects that are ready to mate. The sensitive antennae of insects of the opposite sex can detect as little as one molecule of the pheromone from several miles away. Male and female insects of the same species home in on each other by following the phero-mone "trail." Scientists reasoned that if they released, say, the female pheromone of an insect pest in a part of the forest that contained no female insects of that species, they could attract the male insects to that spot and thus prevent them from mating. Insects make pheromones only in very tiny quantities, however, so a way to synthesize the chemicals was needed.

Ian Weatherstone dropped into Fraser-Reid's office to talk while he was on the Waterloo campus. "I know these things won't be of interest to you," Weatherstone said, "but these are some of the compounds we are working on." He drew diagrams of several molecules. One was the pheromone of the western pine beetle, which was the principal pest of timber regions on the western coast of North America. "This insect causes over half a billion dollars' worth of damage to Canadian trees," Weatherstone told Fraser-Reid.

Weatherstone was sure that the pine beetle pheromone would not interest Fraser-Reid because the compound was not a carbo-hydrate. It belonged to another organic chemical family, the terpenes. But Fraser-Reid, as he recalls, mentally "stood on my head . . . and looked at it the way a sugar chemist would. And I said, 'Hey! There's a highway from sugar to that molecule.'"

Scientists had already found ways to synthesize pheromones, but Fraser-Reid's process offered the advantage of making only the "glove" form of the pheromone molecule that insects could detect (they could not sense the mirror-image form). Fraser-Reid and Weatherstone drew up plans to make the pine beetle phero-mone from glucose within two weeks. Unfortunately, Fraser-Reid remembers, the rest of the story "is not a very happy one." The agency that had promised funds for the project "dragged its feet." Before the project could be completed, Weatherstone left Canada to work for a United States firm, and Fraser-Reid lost contact with the Canadian Forest Service. The project was dropped. Research on using pheromones to control pest insects has continued, but Fraser-Reid has not been involved in it.

In 1980 Fraser-Reid himself left Canada. "I hated to do it," he says. "Canada has been enormously good to me." Several univer-sities in the United States, however, were begging him to join their faculties, and he consented at last to go to the University of Maryland. He worked for a while on synthesizing chemicals that were being tested as possible anticancer drugs. As a chemist, however, Fraser-Reid was not concerned with their biological activity. "I worked on these compounds because they were complex and challenging," he says. In this he differed from Jane Wright, who was more interested in such drugs' medical effects than in their chemistry, and Percy Julian, who sought practical uses for the compounds he made. Like Ernest Just, Fraser-Reid is interested primarily in "pure" rather than applied science.

In 1983 Fraser-Reid moved to Duke University in Durham, North Carolina, where he still teaches and does research as the James B. Duke Professor of Chemistry. There he found that the processes he had worked out for making nonsugar compounds from sugars "turned around at the end and came back to benefit sugars," he says. He has been able to use his earlier ideas to invent new ways to synthesize complex sugar-containing molecules. One of these synthesis methods, which he and his co-workers developed and patented in 1988, is called the n-pentenyl glycoside strategy. It links simple sugars together to make oligosaccharides, which include some of the most important compounds that regulate biological activities. Fraser-Reid says that he and the others in his lab could not have discovered this reaction if they had not branched out into nonsugar areas. "It was a pure case of serendipity," he says—finding one useful thing while looking for another. "That's how most progress in science occurs."

This new strategy allows Fraser-Reid and others to synthesize oligosaccharides more efficiently and economically than before. Some can be made for the first time. Being able to make these chemicals easily will help scientists learn how they work. The process also has provided information about how oligosaccharides break down, which is important in understanding how they work in the body.

Fraser-Reid's work could contribute to medicine because oligosaccharides and other carbohydrates are so important in the body. They make up part of the structure of cells and also are involved in many interactions between cells as well as in internal cell processes such as growth. Carbohydrates combine with proteins and other chemicals to make other important biological molecules.

To give one example of the possible importance of Fraser-Reid's work, it may someday lead indirectly to a vaccine or treatment for AIDS. Oligosaccharides, such as those studied by Fraser-Reid, are found on the outer coat of the virus that causes this terrible disease. The breakdown or "trimming" of these oligosaccharides is one step in the process that activates the virus so that it can invade cells. If scientists learn enough about the way these oligosaccharides break down, Fraser-Reid points out, they might be able to stop the breakdown in some way and thus keep the virus from becoming active.

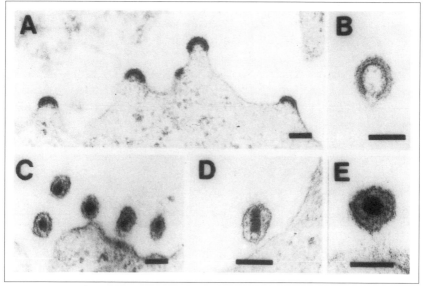

AIDS virus. This deadly virus may someday be inactivated by preventing an oligosaccharide on its surface from breaking down.
(Courtesy *Science* magazine, Vol. 225, 24 August 1984 [Copyright 1984 by American Association for the Advancement of Science] and Jay A. Levy.)

Oligosaccharides and other complex sugar-containing molecules appear on the surfaces of many cells as well as on viruses. They stick up from the cell surfaces "like antennae," Fraser-Reid says. These molecules have unusual shapes that fit the shapes of certain other molecules like two pieces of a jigsaw puzzle, or like a key and a lock. If a molecule that fits one of these receptor molecules comes into contact with it, the two molecules lock together and send a signal to the inside of the cell. Depending on the kinds of molecules involved, the signal causes various activities to occur in the cell. Some receptor molecules detect hormones, such as insulin or cortisone. Others in the brain detect chemicals called neurotransmitters, and the interactions between neurotransmitters and their receptors carry the messages that allow people to move and think. Still other receptor molecules, located on certain blood cells, react with antigens on bacteria or other "foreign" substances. (As Charles Drew learned, reactions between antigens and their receptors are the reason that the blood of someone with one blood type sometimes cannot be transfused into someone with another blood type.) Scientists are only beginning to learn about receptor molecules, and Fraser-Reid's work surely will help them.

Fraser-Reid's work has won several awards in addition to the one from Merck. He won the 1990 Claude S. Hudson Award in carbohydrate chemistry from the American Chemical Society, for example. He also was named a Senior Distinguished United States Scientist by the Alexander von Humboldt Foundation in Germany in 1989. Some writers have even suggested that Fraser-Reid's work in synthesizing nonsugars from sugars and in making oligosaccharides may someday win him the most prestigious scientific award of all, the Nobel Prize. If that happens, Fraser-Reid will be the first black scientist to win the prize.

When asked to name the most personally satisfying aspect of his work, Fraser-Reid does not list any of his scientific achievements. Instead, he cites the "interaction with the young men and young women" who have worked in his laboratory. He values highly the learning experiences he had in the labs of Jones, Lemieux, and Barton, and he tries to help young researchers in his own laboratory gain similar experience. Like George Washington Carver and Charles Drew, Fraser-Reid enjoys teaching as much as research. He is particularly proud of a special program, sponsored by the National Science Foundation, that he initiated at Duke. It allows three high school students and three university undergraduates from minority groups to work with members of the Duke chemistry faculty each summer.

Fraser-Reid believes that talented black scientists today usually will not encounter the problems that held back the academic careers of scientists such as Ernest Just and Percy Julian.

"Science is so universal that if you're good, it's going to be hard to keep you back," he says. "Science is a worldwide culture. My lab is full of people from Spain, England, Sweden—all over." Students should look for a chance to study in laboratories where a variety of creative people are working, he believes. "A student learns more by walking down the corridor of a first-rate lab than from someone teaching, because he learns how people do research."

Chronology

February 23, 1934	Bertram O. Fraser-Reid born in Jamaica
1956	enrolls in Queen's University in Ontario, Canada
1959	receives B.S. degree from Queen's University
1961	receives M.S. degree and goes to laboratory of Raymond Lemieux at University of Alberta
1963	marries Lillian Lawrynyuk
1964	receives his Ph.D. from University of Alberta and goes to England to study in laboratory of Sir Derek Barton
1966	joins faculty of University of Waterloo, near Toronto
1975	publishes method for making nonsugar compounds from sugars; works out process for making pheromones
1977	wins Merck, Sharpe & Dohme award for outstanding contribution to organic chemistry in Canada
1980	leaves Canada and joins faculty of University of Maryland
1983	joins faculty of Duke University in Durham, North Carolina
1988	Fraser-Reid and his coworkers develop n-pentenyl glycoside strategy for making oligosaccharides
1989	Fraser-Reid named a Senior Distinguished United States Scientist by Alexander von Humboldt Foundation

Further Reading

Most of the information in this profile was obtained from interviews with Bertram Fraser-Reid. The author thanks Dr. Fraser-Reid for his courtesy and cooperation.

Bucke, C., and R. A. Rastall. "Synthesizing Sugars by Enzymes in Reverse." *Chemistry in Britain*, July 1990. Provides background information on importance of carbohydrates in the body.

"Driven by Sugar." *Black Enterprise*, February 1990. Brief but informative sketch of Fraser-Reid's life and work.

Edelson, "Scanning the Body Magnetic." *Science 83*, July-August 1983. Provides background information on nuclear magnetic resonance.

Fincher, Jack. "The Bug Wars." *Science Digest*, August 1985. Provides background information on pheromones.

Garegg, Per J. "Artificial Antigens—Prospects for Medicine." *Chemistry in Britain*, July 1990. Provides background information on importance of carbohydrates in the body.

Sharon, Nathan, and Halina Lis. "Carbohydrate-Protein Interactions." *Chemistry in Britain*, July 1990. Provides background information on importance of carbohydrates in the body.

Stuckey, William K. "A Strong and Unusual Nobel Contender." *Leader*, September 14, 1989. Describes Fraser-Reid's life and work, emphasizing the possibility of his winning a Nobel Prize.

Sturgeon, R. A. "Contemporary Carbohydrate Chemistry." *Chemistry in Britain*, July 1990. Provides a brief overview of modern carbohydrate chemistry and defines some terms.

John P. Moon
(1938-   )

John P. Moon. Moon, currently Apple Computer's vice president for peripherals engineering, helped to create devices that store and retrieve data generated by computers.
(Courtesy Apple Computer, Inc.)

A student sits at her computer. She has just finished typing part of a report for school. She wants to save her work so that she can continue writing the report at a later time.

The student types a "save" command on her computer keyboard. She hears a whirring sound, and a moment later the televisionlike screen on the computer's monitor tells her that her file—all of the report that she has typed so far—has been saved. Later, when she wants to work on the report again, she will type in the name of the file and command the computer to retrieve it.

After another whirring sound, the beginning of her file will appear on the monitor screen.

The information in the student's file is stored on, and retrieved from, a disk in the machine. Depending on the kind of computer the student is using, the disk may be a "floppy" disk that the student inserts, or it may be a "hard" disk that remains permanently in place. In either case, the disk is used in a device called a disk drive, which contains electronic equipment that can store data (small bits of information) on and retrieve it from the disk. Most hard disk drives and many floppy disk drives are built into the main case of the computer. Some disk drives, however, are separate devices attached to the computer by a cable.

The student's computer disk has much in common with the rock music cassette in her portable tape player. Both contain data (musical sounds in one case, computer data in the other) that are stored on magnetic material made up of tiny particles of ferrite (iron oxide combined with the oxide of some other magnetizable metal) fixed onto a surface.

The computer's disk drive contains a "head" that, like the play head in the tape recorder, is made partly of magnetic material. The disk head in a modern computer is perhaps a tenth of an inch across. The head in a floppy disk drive contacts the disk material, whereas the head in a hard disk drive rides over the disk on a thin cushion of air. At the computer's "save" command, the data stored in the computer's memory are translated into a series of electric signals that turn a magnetic field in the head on and off. The magnetic signals are transmitted from the head to the disk. When the magnetic field is on, the tiny bits of ferrite on the part of the disk nearest the head line up in the same direction, like iron filings placed next to a magnet. A different magnetic signal makes these magnetic spots or "domains" line up in a different direction. Two forms of signal are enough because all data in a computer ultimately are stored in the form of 1's and 0's, or "ons" and "offs."

The head leaves the magnetic pattern imprinted, in a sense, on the disk. Different files are stored on different parts of the disk. The whirring sound that the student heard when her file was saved was the sound of the motor that moved the disk head to the correct part of the disk. The computer ordered the head to go to the same part of the rapidly spinning disk when the student asked to retrieve her file. In that case the head picked up a series of magnetic signals rather than sending them out. These signals were translated into electric signals, which the computer then "read."

The technology that allows the student to store and retrieve her writing owes much to the work of a black engineer named John Moon. Moon, who works for Apple Computer in Cupertino, California, has made a number of improvements in the design and manufacture of computer disk drive heads and related devices.

———

John P. Moon was born in Philadelphia on July 15, 1938. His father, Perry, was a construction worker. Perhaps John inherited an interest in engineering from his father. Even as a child, he always wanted to know "the way things work." The best way to learn how things work, John Moon thought, was either to build them or to take them apart, and he did a good deal of both. He spent hours in the family basement building model planes and cars. He took apart old radios and then tried to repair them. He also, on one memorable Christmas, took apart the Mickey Mouse watch that his sister had received as a present. Neither his sister nor his father was pleased.

John Moon followed his interest in engineering into college. He received a bachelor of science degree in mechanical engineering from Pennsylvania State University in 1960 and went on to get a master's degree from New York University in 1964.

A lucky accident in 1960 led John Moon to the woman he was to marry. Her name was Cynthia Sharpe. He met her by chance in a restaurant, and they were married three months later. They have three children, Sean, Inga, and Tuesday.

The possibility of working on computers never crossed Moon's mind until 1962, when he was hired by International Business Machines (IBM), then and now one of the leaders in computer manufacturing. IBM at that time was sponsoring a program to recruit young black scientists and engineers, and Bernard Schwartz, the head of the program, decided to "take a chance" on Moon even though Moon knew nothing about computers. Moon, in turn, was willing to take a chance on trying to learn a kind of engineering that he had never done before. In terms of his knowledge of computers, "I'm self-taught, basically," Moon says. "I had to work at this."

Computers in the early 1960s filled whole rooms and were extremely expensive. Only the largest companies had them. The technology used to store data in these "mainframe" computers was very different from today's storage technology, too. Ferrite was just beginning to be used in the heads that stored and retrieved the data on the computers' large disks. Before that time, heads had been made of alternating thin layers of metal and insulating material. This kind of head could store or retrieve only a limited quantity of data in a given amount of space. Heads made of ceramic and ferrite allowed more data to be stored in the same space.

Moon found the new ferrite head technology "fascinating." His greatest interest was in finding ways to manufacture the new heads. The combination of metal and ferrite in the heads required a new kind of bonding, a high-temperature process that in turn needed a new kind of furnace. Moon worked with other engineers to adapt machines and techniques from other industries and develop an efficient way of making the heads. "There was room for all disciplines, mechanical engineers, chemists, physicists, electrical engineers" in making the new heads, he recalls.

Eagerness to learn new things helped Moon advance at IBM. "You find out you don't know, and you're bound to learn," he says. "It just grew over time. Achievement in one part of the business led to another part that I was equally unqualified for, then I'd work at that, and then get into another part, and so on."

In 1970 Moon took a chance on doing something else new: he left IBM and joined several other men who were founding a new company that they called National Micronetics Corporation. He didn't do it because he was excited about becoming part of a new venture, though. "It was mainly because IBM wanted me to move to San Jose!" he says. Because Moon didn't want to leave New York and move to northern California, he agreed to join the Micronetics founders, who had heard about him through mutual friends. They were working out ways to use ferrite in devices that stored data as a permanent part of a computer's memory, and they thought that Moon's experience in working with ferrite disk heads would be useful in helping them figure out how to manufacture the devices. (Computer memory today is stored on silicon chips rather than ferrite "cores.") Moon became the company's engineering director.

In fact, Micronetics ended up making Moon's original specialty, ferrite recording heads. It did very well at it. Like some other successful companies in the computer business, Micronetics grew from four or five men working in a garage to a multimillion dollar business within a few years.

The world of computers was beginning to change in the early 1970s. Until that time, IBM had made most of the computers and attached "peripherals" (devices used with computers, such as disk drives, printers, and monitors) that were used in the United States. At that point, though, a number of small companies began to make peripherals that could be used with IBM computers but were much cheaper than the peripherals that IBM sold. The companies that made disk drives needed ferrite recording heads, and Micronetics grew along with that demand.

Moon found working for a small company to be very different from working for giant IBM. He says he is glad that he started at IBM because the big company gave him a lot of support and many opportunities to learn. But a small company had its own advantages, he found out. "You have lots of control," he says, "and lots of responsibility. In a small company, you have to learn to do for yourself."

Moon might have left IBM because he didn't want to move to California, but his work for Micronetics eventually took him to California anyway. Around 1974 Micronetics bought a company in southern California, in San Diego, that made a specialized type of disk drive, and Moon moved to San Diego as part of the team that took over and managed the smaller company.

Moon enjoyed his work at Micronetics, but after a few years he felt that his career could no longer advance in that company. Searching once more for new and challenging work, therefore, he joined another fairly small company, Tandon Magnetics Corporation. The company had been founded—once again, in a garage—by "Jugi" (pronounced "Juggy") Tandon, a man of Hindu descent whose real first name was too long for his coworkers to pronounce. At the time Moon joined Tandon's company, in 1976, it had about 25 employees. Tandon Magnetics also was in southern California, in a town called Chatsworth.

Tandon became a leader in the next stage of the growth—or perhaps one should say shrinkage—of computers. As the "insides" of computers changed from bulky radio tubes to smaller, more reliable transistors and then to silicon microchips, the computers shrank from room-size to desk-size and even smaller. At the same time they grew both more powerful (able to store more data and perform mathematical operations faster than ever before) and cheaper.

In the mid-1970s the first microcomputers or personal computers began to appear. At first these computers existed only in the form of kits that a few hobbyists built. Compared to the large computers in existence at the time, they could do almost nothing. Nonetheless, the idea of a computer that was cheap enough for almost anyone to afford and small enough to be used on a desk in an office or home attracted many people. Microcomputers slowly became more powerful and easier to use, and companies began selling complete computers instead of kits. The personal computer market mushroomed.

People who used the new computers needed a way to store data beyond the small amount that could be held in the computer's memory (which was erased when the computer was turned off). Data could be stored on magnetic tape cassettes, but a cassette had to be played through until the desired data were reached, just as an audiocassette must be played through to reach a particular song. Some time before, IBM had commercialized small, so-called "floppy" disks coated with magnetic material as a way of storing data. Floppy disks originally had been intended simply as a way for computers to record and store a small amount of data that could be used by technicians who were trying to diagnose problems inside the computer. Inventors such as Al Shugart, however, saw the floppy disk's potential for storing data in personal computers. Shugart invented the 5¼-inch floppy disk, the kind used in most early microcomputers. In a more advanced form, this kind of disk is still used in many computers. (It looks like a slightly shrunken 45-rpm record kept permanently in its jacket.) Floppy disks greatly increased the usefulness of and demand for personal computers because they made it possible to store a relatively large amount of data in a form that could be retrieved quickly for later use.

As the demand for personal computers skyrocketed, so did the demand for floppy disks and the disk drives and disk heads that stored and retrieved data on the disk. At first only one side of a floppy disk could be used to store data because the head in the disk drive could contact only one side. Each disk, therefore, could hold only a fairly small amount of data. Jugi Tandon, however, invented a double-sided disk head that could store and detect data on both sides of a disk. This automatically doubled the disk's capacity. Tandon's type of head is still widely used today.

Tandon's new double-sided disk head soon was in great demand. Moon, as always the practical engineer, helped the Tandon company work out efficient ways to manufacture the new heads. As with the ferrite heads at IBM, he made several advances in this manufacturing process. For example, he worked out a way to make the heads in groups or batches, which was more efficient than making them one at a time. Tandon Magnetics grew tremendously and branched out into making floppy and hard disk drives as well as heads.

Moon was happy at Tandon, but another rising computer giant had other plans for him. By 1980 Apple Computer in northern California, started by inventors Steve Wozniak and Steve Jobs in yet another garage in 1976, was taking over a growing share of the personal computer market. Apple wanted to design and make its own floppy disks and disk drives rather than use those made by Shugart or Tandon. Steve Wozniak had invented a floppy disk controller that was cheaper and easier to use than those currently used because it needed only a single silicon microchip. The disk controller, following instructions from the computer, activates the motor to position the disk head over the spot on the disk where desired data are stored or will be stored. The controller also converts magnetic signals into electronic signals and vice versa.

Apple needed a new kind of disk drive head to go with the controller that "Woz" planned to use. The inventors at Apple looked through literature about disk drive design improvements to see who might help them design such a head. Soon after that, Apple began to pester John Moon about going to work for the company.

The main pesterer was Rod Holt, Apple's chief scientist. Holt began to call Moon at "all kinds of hours," trying to persuade him to join Apple.

Moon at that time had never heard of Apple. He also had no particular desire to leave Tandon. For some time he refused to speak to Holt. Finally, however, Holt caught him at the office one Saturday morning, and the two men talked. The next day, Holt flew to southern California to continue the discussion. Moon in turn agreed to visit Cupertino to meet the people in charge of Apple.

Moon liked the Apple executives, but he was just as adamant as he had been back in his IBM days: he didn't want to move to northern California. He told Apple as much and returned home.

The next day, Holt called again. "Where *do* you want to live?" he asked Moon.

"Where I am," Moon replied.

"Fine," said Holt. "Put us in the head business there."

Apple sent a man down to Thousand Oaks, where Moon lived, to help him set up a plant. The man drove Moon around during Moon's lunch hour to look at possible properties. Only when the building was chosen and leased did Moon finally agree to quit Tandon. "It was an opportunity to do my own thing, so I took it," he says.

Moon headed the Thousand Oaks plant for four years. He designed a disk drive head that worked with Wozniak's new controller. He also helped to design and put into pilot production several other kinds of floppy and hard disk drive heads. During Moon's time there, the plant grew until it had 120 employees.

Moon's fondness for Apple grew too, and finally, around 1984, he was persuaded to join the main company in Cupertino, about half an hour's drive south of San Francisco. After about a year, Moon was given control of the division that made peripheral devices to go with Apple computers. Apple by then had become one of the 500 largest corporations in the United States.

Moon's most interesting project in his new job was working on the disk drive to be used in Apple's new Macintosh computer. Sony, a Japanese company, had developed a drive that could be used with a new size of floppy disk, the 3½-inch disk, that was going to be used in the Macintosh. (Later it was used in many other personal computers as well.) Although this disk was physically smaller, it could hold more data than most 5¼-inch floppies. Encased in a hard plastic shell, it also was better protected against damage than the older style of disk.

The drive that Sony had designed, however, did not work as well as Moon and others hoped it would. Data are stored on computer disks in concentric tracks, something like the tracks or grooves on a phonograph record. The disk head in Sony's drive could not "read" the data tracks near the inside edge of the disk because this part of the disk, where the magnetic material was clamped to the disk spindle, was very stiff. The stiffness meant that the bottom and top disk heads could not read the disk at the same time. Moon, however, worked with Sony to change the design of the heads, the thickness of the disk material, and the way the material was clamped. He found a way to make the inside tracks of the disk usable, thus considerably increasing its data storage capacity. In doing this, he achieved something that "at the time was considered impossible."

Moon recalls his early years of work on the Macintosh fondly, saying that they were perhaps the most personally fulfilling time of his career. "Everybody was involved, the hardware people, the software [programming] people, the visual designers, the mass storage people, and so forth. It was very rewarding, both in terms of personal enrichment and from the point of view of just having fun."

Today, as Apple's vice president for peripherals engineering, John Moon does more administration than research. He continues to take a lively interest in the products that his division puts out, however. At present, he says, the division is concentrating on imaging products. Engineers there are trying to find ways to manipulate images shown on the computer's monitor screen and on printers so that the images will appear as lifelike as possible and also so that the images produced by, say, a color printer will not look too different from the same images seen on a color monitor.

Macintosh computers. These computers are descendants of the original Apple Macintosh computer, for which John Moon helped to design disk drives.
(Courtesy Apple Computer, Inc.)

"There's quite a bit of computation involved in making these images look lifelike," Moon points out. The image on a monitor screen, like that on a television screen or a newspaper photograph, is made up of thousands of tiny dots. The dots on a monitor screen are called pixels. The pixels must be manipulated in complex ways to, for example, keep a curved line in an image smooth when the image is enlarged. Making colors match between monitors and printers also is "a very, very intricate and complex technical problem," involving both hardware (silicon chips and other parts of the computer machinery) and software (programs that tell the computer what to do), Moon explains.

Moon's career, like the careers of Percy Julian and (in a different way) George Washington Carver, has been aimed toward the practical. Moon modestly insists that none of his inventions have made major changes in the computer industry. "I think I've been *around* things that have changed the industry, though," he adds. These include Jugi Tandon's two-sided disk head and Sony's 3½-inch disk drive. Moon says his engineering contributed to making these important inventions "even better" and easier to manufacture efficiently. Perhaps he will "be around" other important inventions in the future and make them better as well, for one of his ambitions is to go into business for himself in a few years. He doesn't say what he will make, except that it will not be disk drive heads. As always, Moon looks forward to the challenge of trying something new.

Like Jane Wright and Bertram Fraser-Reid, John Moon does not feel that being black has held back his career, at least not in ways that he was aware of. "I'm sure there were some people that didn't like me because I was black, or who questioned my ability because of that," he says, but he refused to let their attitude affect him. He feels that they, in turn, were willing to tolerate him because his skills helped the companies he was involved with make money.

The most important thing that young people of any race who are interested in science or engineering can do, Moon believes, is

> pick something they like and are willing to work at, that makes them feel, "Gosh, this is interesting, I want to do this and learn more about it." That leads to being good at it. Be good at what you do, and don't let people's attitudes slow you down. Look for love among your family and friends, not your coworkers.

Moon thinks that a young person's, especially a young black person's, chance for achievement is likely to be greater with a small company than with a large one. Large companies are more likely to hire someone simply because he or she is black, without giving the person a real chance to contribute talent or expertise to the company. Such a practice is tokenism, which Moon despises:

> Even if you sit on the Board of Directors, if you're there to be the black person on the board, and they turn to you when an issue about black employees or clients comes up but you're not considered as contrib-

*uting to the overall company bottom line, that's tokenism. The goal
is not to be a professional black. You're a professional person who
happens to be black. That's a different thing.*

Small companies cannot afford to hire people only as tokens,
Moon believes. In such companies, "contribution is going to be
much more important than the color of your skin." These companies, even more than large ones, are likely to be extremely interested in "the bottom line"—the overall profitability of the
company—and anyone who can help the company make money
will probably be treated well. "If you're contributing," Moon
emphasizes, "you play."

Chronology

━━━━━

July 15, 1938	John P. Moon born in Philadelphia
1960	receives B.S. degree from Pennsylvania State University; marries Cynthia Sharpe
1962	goes to work for IBM
1964	receives M.S. degree from New York University
1970	goes to work for National Micronetics Corporation
1974	moves to southern California
1976	joins Tandon Magnetics Corporation
1980	Apple Computer hires Moon to run new plant for making disk drive heads in southern California
1984	Moon moves to Apple's headquarters in northern California
1985	is put in charge of Apple's peripheral devices division, begins work on disk drive for Macintosh computer
1990	begins work on imaging products for computers

Further Reading

━━━━━━━━━━━

Most of the information in this profile was obtained from the author's interviews with John Moon. The author wishes to thank Mr. Moon and his assistant, Rita Taylor, for their courtesy and cooperation. The author also wishes to thank Harry Henderson and Hal Heydt for background information on disk technology.

Augarten, Stan. *Bit by Bit: An Illustrated History of Computers.* New York: Ticknor and Fields, 1984. Provides background information on the history of computers.

Gremillion, Lee L., and Philip J. Pyburn. *Computers and Information Systems in Business: An Introduction.* New York: McGraw-Hill, 1988. Includes information on how disks and disk drives are used to store and retrieve computer data.

"Master of the Hard Drive." *Black Enterprise*, February 1990. Brief but informative sketch of Moon's life and work.

Index

Bold numbers indicate main headings

A

Adrenal glands 42, 49
Aero-Foam (fire-smothering foam) 47
African Research Foundation 72
Agriculture, Southern—*See South, agriculture in*
AIDS 80–81, 89
Alcohol (automobile fuel) 15
Alkaloids 84
Alkylating agents 71–73
American College of Surgeons 10, 69
American Red Cross 60–61, 64
Antibodies 58–59
Anticancer drugs—*See Cancer— chemotherapy*
Antigens 58–59, 90
Apple Computer, Inc. 96, 100–102
Arthritis 41–42, 48, 50

B

Banneker, Benjamin x
Barton, Sir Derek 84, 90
Basic Methods for Experimenting on Eggs of Marine Animals (Just book) 33
Biology of the Cell Surface, The (Just book) 35–37
Black colleges and universities viii, ix, 33
Blacks
    difficulties faced as scientists vii, ix, xi, 91, 103–104
    education of vii–viii
    reputation as scientists x–xi
Blanchard, William 43, 45–46
Blood
    banks xi, 55, 59–62, 64, 76

cells, red 56–60
cells, white 68, 71
plasma xi, 55, 59–62, 64
preservation 59–61
serum 56–59
transfusions 2, 56–59, 61, 90
types 56–61, 90
Bouchet, Edward vii
Brazil 15
Britain, Blood for, program 60–62

C

Cancer 68,70–77, 81, 83, 88
    chemotherapy 68, 70–77, 88
    leukemia 68, 71
Cancer Research Foundation 70–72
Carbohydrates 81–85, 87–90
Carbolic acid 3
Carver, George Washington viii, x, xi, **14–27**, 33, 37–38, 46, 50, 64, 69, 90, 103
    awards and honors 23
    chronology 26
    criticism of 24
    education of 16
    farmers, educating 20–21
    influence of 24–25
    museum and foundation 23
    peanuts, products from, creation by 20–23
    reputaton of 21–24
    southern agriculture, plans to help 18–20, 22
    slave birth of 15
    Tuskegee Institute, teaching at 17, 20–21
Casein 46–47
Cell surface (membrane) 28, 32, 35, 37

Index

Chemistry, organic—*See Organic chemistry*
Chemotherapy, cancer—*See Cancer—chemotherapy*
Chemurgy 22
Chicago, University of 30–31, 33
Civil War 15
Columbia University (New York City) 58–62
Computers 83, 94–103
    disk controllers 100–101
    disk drive heads 95, 97–101, 103
    disk drives 95, 98–101, 103
    disks 95, 99, 101
    imaging on 102–103
    memory 97–98
    monitor 102
    personal 98–99
Cortexolone 49
Cortisone xi, 42, 48–50, 90
Cotton 19
Cross-matching 58–59
Cytoplasm 28, 35, 37

D

DDT 86
DePauw University (Greencastle, Indiana) 43, 45–46
Disk drives—*See Computers—disk drives*
Disks, computer—*See Computers—disks*
Drew, Charles Richard viii, ix, xi, 11, 33, 37, **54–66**, 69, 76, 90
    athletic career 55–56, 62
    awards and honors 63
    blood bank work 59–61, 64
    blood plasma work 60, 64
    chronology 65
    early years 55
    education of 55–56, 58–59
    influence of 64
    teaching of surgeons 58, 62–64
DuBois, W. E. B. viii
Duke University (Durham, N.C.) 88, 90

E

Ecology 24
Ectoplasm 35, 37
Egg cell 28–29, 31–32

F

Ferrite 95–99
Fertilization, process of 28–29, 31–32, 35
Ford, Henry 23
Fraser-Reid, Bertram O. ix, xi, 38, **80–93**, 103
    awards and honors 85, 90
    carbohydrates, work with 81–90
    chronology 92
    early years 81–82
    education of 82–84
    influence of 89–90
    n-pentenyl glycoside strategy development 88
    nuclear magnetic resonance use 83–84
    petroleum compounds, synthesis from sugars 85
    pheromone synthesis 86–87
    pure compounds, synthesis 85, 87
    sugars, synthesis of nonsugars from, 84–88, 90
Freedmen's Hospital (Washington, D.C.) 7–10, 30, 62–63, 69
Fructose 82, 84

G

Genes 28, 35, 37
Glaucoma (eye disease) 44–45
Glidden Company 46–47, 50
Glioblastoma (brain tumor) 73
Glucose 82, 87

H

Hall, George C. 10
Heart surgery—*See Surgery—heart*
Hormones 42, 48, 50, 71, 76, 90

Howard University (Washington, D.C.) 7, 11, 30, 33–34, 36–37, 44–45, 55–56, 58, 61–63

I

IBM—*See International Business Machines Corp.*
Immune system 48, 50, 58, 68
Insect pests, controlling 81, 86–87
International Business Machines Corp. (IBM) 96–100
Interracial hospitals, first 5, 11, 69
Iowa State College (Ames) 16–17

J

Jefferson, Thomas vii
Jones, J. K. N. 82–83, 90
Julian, Percy Lavon viii–xi, 33, **41–53**, 63–64, 76, 81, 84, 86, 90, 103
  awards and honors 50
  chronology 51–52
  cortisone synthesis 48–49
  early years 42–43
  education of 43–44
  Glidden Co., work at 46–50
  hormone synthesis 48–49
  influence of 50
  physostigmine synthesis 44–46
  soybeans, syntheses from 46–49
  teaching 43–46
Just, Ernest Everett viii, ix, **28–40**, 43–45, 50, 63, 88, 90
  cell surface, research on 35
  chronology 39
  early years 29
  education of 29–30
  European research 34–36
  grants received by 34
  Howard University, teaching at 30, 33–34, 36
  influence of 37–38
  Marine Biological Laboratory, research at 31–34

Spingarn Medal received by 32–33

K

Kaiser Wilhelm Institute (Berlin, Germany) 34
Kenya 14, 72

L

Landsteiner, Karl 56–59
Legumes 19, 24, 46
Lemieux, Raymond U. 83–84, 90
Leukemia—*See Cancer*
Lillie, Frank R. 30–31, 33, 35, 37, 44
Lister, Joseph 3–4
Loeb, Jacques 32–33

M

McGill University (Montreal, Canada) 56, 58, 61
Macintosh (computer) 101
Magnetic field 83, 95
Magnetic resonance imaging (MRI)—*See Nuclear magnetic resonance*
Marine Biological Laboratory (Woods Hole, Mass.) 30–35, 37
Mayo Clinic (Rochester, Minn.) 42
Mechanists 35
Meharry Medical College (Nashville, Tenn.) 9, 11, 56
Microcomputers—*See Computers—personal*
Micronetics Corp. 97–98
Mithramycin (anticancer drug) 73
Monosaccharides 82–83
Moon, John P. ix, **94–106**
  Apple Computer, work at 100–102
  chronology 105
  disk drive heads, manufacture 97–101, 103
  early years 96
  education of 96

Index

IBM, work at 96–97
imaging, computer, work on 102–103
influence of 103
Micronetics Corp., work at 97–98
race, effects on career 103–104
Tandon Magnetics, work at 98–100
Mycology (study of fungi) x, 16

N

National Association for the Advancement of Colored People (NAACP) 23, 32, 50, 63
National Inventors' Hall of Fame 50
National Medical Association 8, 76
Nereis—See Sandworm
"New South" movement 22
New York Medical College 69, 73
Nitrogen mustard 71, 73
NMR—*See Nuclear magnetic resonance*
N-pentenyl glycoside strategy 88
Nuclear magnetic resonance (NMR) 83–84
Nursing school, black, first 4–5

O

Oligosaccharides 83, 88–90
Organic chemistry 44, 81, 84–85, 87

P

Pasteur, Louis 3
Peanuts 19–22, 46
Personal computers—*See Computers—personal*
Petroleum 81, 85
Pheromones 86–87
Plasma—*See Blood—plasma*
Polychemotherapy 76–77
Progesterone (hormone) 48

Provident Hospital (Chicago) 5, 8–11, 69

R

Receptors 89–90
Red Cross—*See American Red Cross*
Roosevelt, Franklin D. 23
Rosenwald, Julius 34, 38

S

Sandworm (*Nereis*) 32
Schools, movable 20–21
Scudder, John 58–60, 64
Serum—*See Blood—serum*
Shock 6, 54–55, 58, 60
Shugart, Al 99, 100
Slavery vii, 15
Sony Corp. 101, 103
South, agriculture in xi, 17–20, 22
Soybeans 42, 44, 46–48, 50
Spaeth, Ernst 44
Sperm cell 28–29, 31–32
Spingarn Medal (given by NAACP) 23, 32–33, 38, 50, 63
Spleen 9
Steroids 48, 84
Sterols 44, 48, 50
Sucrose 82, 84
Sugars—*See Carbohydrates*
Surgeons, black, training 4, 9, 55, 62–64
Surgery
    antiseptic 3–5
    heart 2, 5–6
    modern 1–2
    19th-century 2–3
    spleen 9
Sweet potatoes 19, 21, 23

T

"Talented tenth" viii
Tandon, "Jugi" 98–100, 103
Tandon Magnetics Corp. 98–101
Terpenes 84, 87
Testosterone 48
Thalidomide 85

Tissue culture test for anticancer drugs 74–75
Transfusions—*See Blood—transfusions*
Triethylenemelamine (TEM) (anticancer drug) 72
Tuskegee Institute viii, 17, 19–23

V

Vitalists 35

W

Washington, Booker T. vii–viii, 17, 20–21, 23
Waterloo, University of (Canada) 84, 86–87
Williams, Daniel Hale viii, **1–13**, 30, 63–64, 69
    chronology 12
    conflicts in later years 10
    early years 2–3
    education of 3–4
    Freedmen's Hospital, chief surgeon at 7–9
    heart surgery by 5–6
    influence of 11
    Meharry Medical College, lectures at 9
    National Medical Association founding 8

Provident Hospital founding 4–5
    spleen surgery by 9
Winged bean 15, 24
Wozniak, Steve 100–101
Wright, Jane Cooke ix, **67–79**, 88, 103
    Africa, work in 72
    awards and honors 76
    cancer chemotherapy, work in 71–77
    Cancer Research Foundation, work for 69–70
    chronology 78
    dosage of anticancer drugs, work on ways to determine 75–76
    education of 69
    family history 68–69
    influence of 76
    mithramycin, testing of 73
    tissue culture testing of anticancer drugs 74–75
    university posts 72–73
Wright, Louis Tompkins 68–70,

Y

Yams 42, 50